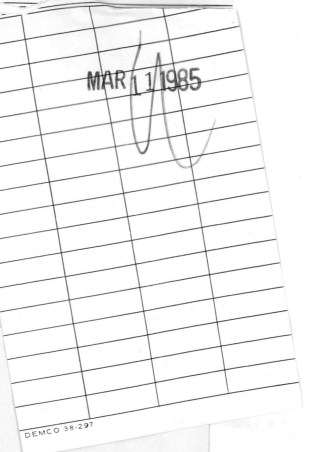

HOUSING FOR THE AGED

This book is published by Teakfield Limited in association with the Joint Unit for Research on the Urban Environment (JURUE) of the University of Aston in Birmingham. It is one of a series of research monographs reporting work sponsored by a range of agencies in both the public and private sectors.

JURUE is a multi-disciplinary research organisation of planners, social scientists, engineers and architects undertaking applied, policy orientated research in the fields of environmental planning and design and urban environmental studies.

The monographs are produced under the general editorship of Frank Joyce and an editorial board comprised of:-

D.M. Johnson	Lecturer in Urban Environmental Studies, JURUE Co-ordinator of Planning Studies
F.E. Joyce (Chairman)	Head of JURUE, Reader in Urban Environmental Studies
E.A. Rose	Professor of Planning and Head of the Department of Architectural, Planning and Urban Studies
H.E. Williams	Deputy Head of JURUE

Housing for the aged

EDGAR A. ROSE

SAXON  HOUSE

Published by Saxon House, Teakfield Limited, Westmead, Farnborough, Hampshire, England.

ISBN   0 566 00217 5

 British Library Cataloguing in Publication Data

Rose, Edgar
    Housing for the aged.
    1. Aged - England - Dwellings
    2. Architecture, Domestic - England
    I. Title
    728.3   NA7195.A4

    ISBN 0-566-00217-5

Printed by David Green (Printers) Ltd, Kettering, Northamptonshire

Contents

Chapter 3   The warden survey

Chapter 4   The tenant survey

Chapter 5   Conclusions and recommendations

Appendices   Part I

Preface

In spite of its fourteen years' experience of providing nationwide accommodation for the elderly, the Committee of Management of the Hanover Housing Association, ever seeking to achieve the highest standards, conscious of the risk of failing to be outward looking and desirous of undertaking any experiments which might be feasible and beneficial to its present and future tenants, decided to commission this study, which it was enabled to do with the aid of a substantial grant from The National Corporation for the Care of Old People, to which body it owes its origin.

It is inevitable when an outside agency conducts a detailed study such as this that criticisms and adverse comments from both wardens and tenants must result, especially as they were specifically invited. Indeed, were they not to have been invited and made, the resultant Report which follows would have been of little value to the Committee of Hanover or to that of any other charitable housing association with similar objects. They were, therefore, welcome. However, as the footnotes indicate, most, if not all the subjects of adverse comment had been rectified.

In common with all other charitable housing associations, Hanover's activities are restricted by constraints imposed by legislation and by the interpretation of those constraints by the Department of the Environment and the Housing Corporation, and it is important that this Report provides some evidence on which representations may be justified aimed at achieving some change in or relaxation of those constraints.

What is said in the Conclusion of Chapter 2 et seq is accepted by the Committee as justification for the commissioning of the study as well as for the publication of its findings.

L.A. Hackett, OBE.,
Chairman, Hanover Housing Association

1 Introduction

PERSPECTIVES

Since this study was commissioned in late 1975, much has changed. The economic climate has worsened. The financial resources available to housing associations have been cut back. The acceptance of high standards represented by Parker Morris recommendations, made during a period in which norms, values, expectations and forecasts of economic and demographic growth were very different - and wrong - are now being questioned by many social and housing policy experts.

The reasons are complex, but at the risk of simplification, the argument is that it may be better to spend dwindling resources differently in respect of various 'goods', than have previously seemed sensible. If less resources are to be made available and energy costs continue to rise, then it is not unreasonable to postulate the advantages of reductions in certain standards if the 'trade-off' results in dwellings that cost less to heat, and are more satisfactory to old people with dwindling resources of their own.

From government's point of view, public finance must be more effectively deployed in pursuit of explicit policy objectives. The consumer is similarly concerned with these changes and their consequences. He or she likewise expects value for money even when it is necessary to adapt to the harsher realities of today.

It has been taken as axiomatic that this study had to proceed from an understanding of some of the problems which an ageing population presents for government, for Associations such as Hanover, for ordinary people and the aged themselves. In this sense, the report may be viewed as a discussion document dealing with desirable standards of housing designed specifically for elderly people who are sufficiently healthy and mobile to live independently in self-contained dwelling units. It, therefore, may be of assistance to a wider audience than Hanover Housing Association; encouraging debate on appropriate policies for meeting the problems discussed, and assisting those intending to organise, finance, design, manage or build housing for the active elderly.

In no sense should the report be regarded as a manual of rules for Hanover Housing Association or anyone else. It will become apparent to the discerning reader that local conditions point to final modifications of design and interpretations of appropriate criteria.

Because the study looks at relevant literature and research as well as at Hanover Housing Association schemes, it is necessary to appreciate that the study allows the reader to learn about the general state of research and to identify some of the gaps which exist. Similarly, it is possible to learn about the generally accepted practices which are adopted in this country. The literature reviewed allows general comparisons to be made between Hanover's practices and those made by others.

It has been appreciated from the outset that the constraints under which Hanover and other voluntary housing associations work vis a vis national legislation and housing categories explains or helps to explain why certain things are, or are not, provided in elderly people's dwellings. If institutional arrangements hinder innovation or limit the introduction of experimental features then recommendations for change may need to be made. The fact that Hanover may be prevented from undertaking some perceived improvement because it breaks the rules deserves examination if only to establish whether and in which circumstances that perceived improvement should be made. Empirical study of the character we have undertaken is valuable in making a case for changing decision rules.

In addition, the results of survey provide an overall picture of the degree to which the schemes are acceptable to the wardens and tenants in them at this point of time. The scope and results of the empirical study are limited necessarily by constraints imposed by terms of reference, resources and time available. But within those self-imposed limitations, it is possible to order results in such a way that they respond to the need to make:

(i)   recommendations for housing schemes for the elderly of a general nature
(ii)   recommendations for Hanover Housing Association of a general nature
(iii)   recommendations on points of detail of a general nature
(iv)   recommendations on specific design features in Hanover Housing schemes
(v)   recommendations relating to unique/discrete schemes.

The general satisfaction with dwellings and schemes is perhaps the most important valuable and reassuring result of the study from Hanover Housing Association's view. But then the study has examined attitudes of a given population and there are inherent limitations in the use of this approach which need to be pointed out.

There is little doubt that special design considerations must continue to play an important part to compensate for the infirmities of old age, if ease, comfort and dignity are to be attributes of growing old. Nevertheless, the study reveals old people wanting to be 'where the action is' as one writer has put it.(1) Ease of access to public facilities, services, district centres and central areas is high on the list of priorities. Accessibility to visiting friends and relatives requires a good location with the benefits of public transportation. High land values have militated against locations in such prime positions, but with the introduction of the Community Land Act and the growing emphasis on retaining people in the inner areas of cities, there is scope for an increasing number of schemes, some of them experimental, being built in such locations. The approach of the housing associations to providing homes for old people has been cautious and as conventional as any building society. This may be justified by reference to consumer preference but market criteria alone are inadequate in considering the wider problems of an ageing population and the existence within it of a wider stratum that may be able to benefit from housing association independent housing. Current practice has favoured small units either for a single person or for a husband and wife. There are very few experimental schemes. There is growing evidence that with more old people, changing life-styles and attitudes, the philosophy of single accommodation should be re-examined and alternatives reviewed to provide for greater flexibility. If more old people seek independence and the State wishes to reduce to a minimum, for good health, psychological and economic reasons, the number of old people living in institutions, then the most interesting developments could be in the direction of multi-use of scarce or expensive facilities coupled with flexible and adaptive old people's schemes allowing a variety of dwelling sizes. For example, two, three or four person dwelling sizes may well be acceptable to elderly people, friends and relatives wishing to share accommodation and facilities. Variety in dwelling size within one scheme could be achieved by skilful design so that minimum adaptation could vary the mix of unit sizes over time. In addition, the size of schemes overall, the juxtaposition of schemes in relation to medical and other social services deserves much closer study.

The recommendations for experimental schemes which would meet some of the more detailed descriptions or criteria found in this report could improve the quality of living for the elderly. In some cases the quality of an attribute of environmental satisfaction becomes the critical factor. The level and cost of heating has become such a factor. The 'trade-off' between this factor and others has not been measured in this study, but the example is both highly relevant and topical.

Whilst no one believes that building costs can be kept below those generally applied to equivalent residential construction, the introduction of an approach to design which was manifestly concerned with understanding preferences as well as attitudes to existing accommodation, would lead directly to ascertaining what 'goods' tenants or prospective tenants would be prepared to trade-off. In this approach, good design is seen, inter alia, as cost-effective producing a high level of satisfaction and not necessarily costing more than so-called bad design. Above all we need to see a more sensitive appreciation of the needs and aspirations of old people

4

reflected in the practical activities of sponsoring agencies such as Hanover, designers and administrators concerned with co-ordinating the various services for the aged.

PROBLEMS OF AN AGEING POPULATION

Policy considerations

If we agree with C. Wright Mills (2) that social research of any kind is advanced by ideas and is only disciplined by fact, it will be evident that it is essential to recognise the importance of ideas and policies which have prevailed to date. They constitute powerful constraints on the freedom of action of those occupying key roles in the provision of sheltered housing, profoundly influencing design processes, locational and management factors.

For 18 years it has been Government policy to keep as many old people and maintain as many aged sick as possible in the community.(3) The primary consideration in the retention of this policy for so long a period is the threat to the National Health Service posed by the ever increasing numbers of old people. Whatever the merits of domiciliary care, economic forces and the preferences of old people themselves conspire together to underline that sheltered housing is becoming more and more necessary and desirable.

We have tried to maintain a logical connection between such ideas and policies and our more detailed investigations of Hanover Housing Association's schemes. Our conclusions suggest that the facts, whether about levels of satisfaction and preference scores on the one hand, or about the performance of heating systems, noise and alarm systems on the other, are not startling, new or entirely unexpected; there were few surprises here not least because a previous study carried out for Hanover Housing Association went into considerable detail on matters of detailed design within the dwelling.(4) What is more significant is that evidence, derived from the research literature and the responses from wardens and those living in the schemes, is interpreted in ways which reflect the significantly different situation which exists today and is likely to continue for as far ahead as is

5

relevant for us to consider here.

Demographic trends

There are about $6\frac{1}{2}$ million people in England over the age of 65 years ($13\frac{1}{2}$ per cent of the population). This figure has been increasing by about 100,000 p.a. It is expected to stabilise at about 7 million by the year 2000, but the numbers over 75 will increase by one third, and those over 85 by one half.

It has been suggested that by 1990 old people could be occupying as much as 80 per cent of non-psychiatric beds and about 92 per cent of non-maternity beds for women. These estimates are real. The people are alive and are in their fifties and sixties at the present time. It is evident that many more people will need to be maintained in their own homes.

Between 1965 and 1995 the rate of increase in elderly population aged 65 and over will decline dramatically. But this group as a percentage of the total population will rise from 12.2 per cent (1965) to 14.4 per cent (1995). This represents a slow down to the turn of the century. The problem of resources will increase, and of greater significance when considering costs to the rest of society are the over 75's and over 85's. With these groups, the rapid growth we have recently seen in the over 65's has yet to come. In effect, the next ten years is the critical period because the 1965-75 bulge will work its way through to 1975-85. Between 1975 and 1985 the group of over 75's will grow by over 20 per cent not only in absolute terms, but as a proportion of the total population. This equals a 2 per cent growth per year or an extra 50,000 each year. And indeed by the turn of the century well over 1 per cent of us will be over 85 years of age and there are crude indications that the future pattern is likely to be one of heavy dependence with women predominating. We know that at the age of 65 women can expect 15 more years of life whereas men can only expect 12. There are twice as many divorced or widowed women aged 75+.

In the words of a former Minister of State for Health, (5)

6

"There is far too little understanding of the significance of this dramatic demographic change. As yet social policy expenditure priorities have not responded by a matching switch of relating spending priorities from cash provision into care provision for the elderly."

The cost of care

Over seventy voluntary agencies took part in Age Action Year 1976 throughout the UK. This is one of a number of indications of the importance and recognition that is now being given to the problems of an ageing rather than a growing population. This represents a real and increasing diversion of a far higher proportion of the gross national product to the elderly than hitherto.

About 15 per cent of the total UK Health and Social Service Budget is used mainly for services to the elderly and handicapped. The elderly are major users of other services. Probably a third of the expenditure is currently used on treatment and care of the over 65's. These services include in summary:

(i)   The Home Help Service
(ii)   The Meals Service (38 million in a year; 20 million in 1969)
(iii)   Home nurses
(iv)   Chiropody service
(v)   Day centres (14,000 places - 10,000 in 1972)
(vi)   Old People's Homes (maintained by local government)
(vii)   Departments of geriatric medicine (the aged occupy a growing proportion of beds in our other hospitals).

Given the high running costs of day centres, for example, and the distribution of the population making the most use of such accommodation, it will become necessary, and arguably more cost-effective, to provide more modest facilities using adapted buildings, relying on greater voluntary assistance and self-help.

There is a strong concensus supported by the evidence that more resources must be directed to older pensioners in the form of services. Government believes that with advancing

7

age, generally speaking, services become more important and cash income less so.

Tenure, allocation and access

The general characteristics and distribution and allocation of the existing housing stock are highly relevant in terms of policy and priorities. The trend towards renewal and smaller houses means that the children not only move away from the immediate neighbourhood, they have rarely the room to accommodate older relatives. We know that a quarter of the over 65's have no children to assist them in time of need. Access becomes more and more relevant a concept paradoxically during a period that despite our attempts to prevent low density sprawl, has witnessed increased mobility, longer journeys to work and more dispersed patterns of living. The energy crisis and the cost of transport has introduced a new range of factors with the provision of homes for the aged. But the evidence from the aged themselves demonstrates that they cherish their independence and human dignity above all else. They are less different from other groups than they have been represented to be. Perhaps this wish for independence should be the most highly valued attribute in any humanistic calculus we may attempt.

In 1975 there were about 110,000 old people in local authority homes for the elderly and the physically handicapped. The rate of increase is slowing. There is a move to smaller homes and the average age is increasing. Inevitably, with an ageing group, disabilities - physical and mental - have been increasing. This has serious implications for staffing and the need for, and dearth of, longitudinal studies of behavioural response to varied designed environments and specific alternative provisions. If we are to make any fundamental progress in purposefully improving our design solutions and, perhaps of even greater importance, adapting our existing building stock to meet changing needs and relatively smaller budgets, then painstaking observations and measures are required of people's responses to physical change over time.

Apart from local authority provision and direct administrative provisions by health and personal services, the

8

voluntary housing agencies in the UK play an important and increasing role in meeting housing need. Special housing associations such as Hanover (see Appendix II) supply large numbers of suitable and special housing for old people with a warden. Our desk studies and specific research findings reinforce the widely accepted view of practitioners and policy analysts that this provision must be provided within a framework of adequate supporting domiciliary health and social services, and this will undoubtedly require closer co-operation and social planning between local authorities to avoid fragmented responses from different agencies - within an authority and between authorities and agencies public and private.(6)

Implications for research

Our approach to the specific research focussed on the needs of old people as perceived by themselves and the wardens who it transpired had needs of their own which in part affected their efficiency and commitment to their job. We proceeded from the explicit assumption that we did not know what was best for them. We assumed that agencies would become increasingly cost conscious and it seemed evident that the standards, guidelines and tests that Hanover and other associations adopted and generally applied - another area for detailed research - were by definition normative and in no sense directly measurable. They were for the most part based on expectations about the future, not least rates of economic growth and projections of wealth and living standards that are now seen as unrealistic.

TERMS OF REFERENCE AND PURPOSE OF STUDY

The Hanover Housing Association had already commissioned an earlier study which had looked at some of the first schemes which have been built and it appeared to us from the terms of their first note on a 'Proposed Feasibility Study of Housing Design for the Elderly', (Appendix IV) that it would be necessary to make some assessment of the extent to which the schemes built since that time - and a large number have been built - had been successful. We were especially interested in the wardens' and tenants' perceptions of what constituted satisfaction in a scheme or dwelling.

The Association stated that it was:

"anxious to incorporate and try out, in its housing schemes for the elderly, whatever experimental features seem likely to have promise ... with the support of the National Corporation for the Care of Old People (it decided) to promote a feasibility study, on which it is hoped a policy of sound experimental work can be based ...."

They saw the objectives as bringing together any existing information and ideas on 'experiments' and 'other work' relevant to special housing for the elderly and wanted some assessment made of the feasibility of the Association carrying out such work and of the possible benefit to Hanover and for housing policies generally of experimental features and design.

We recognised from the outset that these were very general aims and that some attempt must be made to specify what would be studied. The value of controlled experiments in providing specialised facilities in buildings was not in dispute. The difficulty lay in the virtual absence of such schemes. Hanover was itself a pioneer in the field and its officers were the first to point out the many constraints which operated in practice. We accepted it as axiomatic that institutional and financial constraints inhibited experiment whilst the application of new products was largely prevented by the costs which would be involved. Accordingly, Hanover was asked for and provided an additional note listing some of the questions they considered important enough to include in the study (Appendix IV).

It will be evident from Appendix IV that the emphasis was clearly on the experimental and the extent to which the use and performance of buildings and materials, the design of specific features and components was satisfactory. The list was a long one but could easily have been longer. Many of the problems which might arise in practice could be particular to any one scheme and the result of a uniqueness derived from specific local conditions and design characteristics. Moreover, many problems of construction

10

and design were not peculiar to old people's homes and were the subject of major research effort by the Building Research Station and many other research organisations. In any event, there was at that time no comprehensive bibliography or register of research into old people's dwellings so that the identification of gaps in the research effort could only be identified after knowing reasonably satisfactorily the character and extent of ongoing research in Great Britain.(7)

It seemed essential, therefore, to carry out a desk study which would attempt to present an overall picture of the 'state of the art' - a position statement which would at least identify important work that need not be replicated and which could be useful for housing associations generally, and Hanover in particular.

We were also influenced by the need to make some assessment of the kind of detailed work it was feasible for Hanover or others to carry out; it was evident that whilst Hanover wanted practical results which could be acted upon quickly within existing legal, administrative and financial constraints, some of these constraints might prove insurmountable.

It seemed that any feasibility study could be directed either at short-run objectives (easy to implement recommendations relating to Hanover's design standards and instructions without delving too deeply into broader considerations and behavioural and psychological aspects), or at medium-term objectives (considering more fundamental and basic questions that could arise over a longer time horizon). In practice, the apparent choice between a pragmatic, short-term physical design exercise and the medium-term behavioural approach, is itself too simplistic, and we have tried to reconcile both time horizons and categories of problem within the study.

We were also anxious to identify 'mismatches' between the housing (and environment) and the tenants. We were conscious that tenants grew older and that as they did so, particularly old people, their needs changed and they used space and facilities differently. We knew that a theoretical research scheme that would throw light on this problem was certainly possible, but not very practical at this stage.

It may be appreciated that the research strategy was orientated explicitly towards the needs of the consumer and the general aim was to establish which problems and issues were perceived as important by the users of the schemes. Within this frame, the Association's terms of reference and design requirements were considered and pursued as far as we were able within the limitations imposed by time and resources available to an initial study.

STAGES AND STRUCTURE OF THE STUDY

The study, which was planned to take between nine and ten months to complete, began in January 1976. An Interim Report was completed in April and was discussed with the Management Committee of Hanover Housing Association. The advice and criticism which was received proved to be of considerable value in the subsequent stages of the work. The literature and research review, together with the selective bibliography which together comprise Appendices I and II of Part II were substantially complete at the same time and were also made available to the Management Committee for observations. The Interim Report and the many tables which it contains is not reproduced, but Chapter 3 summarises its contents and provides a full account of its findings. The literature and research review has been amended to meet several criticisms on points of detail and a small number of useful North American titles has been added to the selected bibliography which now comprises 122 items.

The structure of this report comprises an introductory Chapter, followed by Chapter 2 which sets out in summary form the research findings, conclusions and recommendations. The first two chapters, therefore, provide an overview of the feasibility study and its recommendations. The remaining chapters and appendices are divided into Parts I and II. Part I presents an account of the field study of Hanover's housing schemes which covers firstly the postal questionnaires to the wardens of 125 schemes and the subsequent follow up interview questionnaire survey with a sample of tenants in ten selected schemes. Twenty five selected tables; a note on

12

Hanover Housing Association and the voluntary housing movement; an explanatory note on, and copies of the questionnaires used; and Hanover's terms of reference are presented as appendices.

Part II comprises a survey of relevant literature and research, and a selected bibliography. This work provides an overview of relevant published literature and research in progress and identifies the development and direction of, and gaps in, research.

ACKNOWLEDGEMENTS

Whilst the opinions, views and recommendations expressed in this report are my own, I acknowledge the considerable help and advice of many people.

Firstly, postgraduate students in my Department; Simon Cane, who has worked as research assistant on the study from its inception; my thanks are due to him for the painstaking work which went into the design of questionnaires and the Desk Study; the bulk of the drafting of both Interim Report and Desk Study was borne by him; Clive Latter, who carried on the work in the final stages as a part-time assistant, organised the tenant survey and the processing of results in tabular form; and finally, the team that spent part of their Easter vacation 1976 interviewing tenants.

Secondly, the officers of Hanover have been helpful and patient in responding to our various requests and their assistance and advice has been valuable. In particular I would like to thank Mr. P.J. Simpson, FCIA, Hanover's General Manager, Mr. H.W. Mellor, BSc (Econ), Secretary of the National Corporation for the Care of Old People, and other members of Hanover's Management Committee, not least for their constructive remarks and criticisms of the Interim Report.

Thirdly, Tom Muir, MSc, ARIBA, a former postgraduate student of mine and now Principal Lecturer in Birmingham Polytechnic School of Architecture, who was co-author of the previous study undertaken for Hanover, has made helpful suggestions during the course of this work.

Fourthly, I would like to thank my own University of Aston who made it possible for me to undertake a short visit to Canada and USA with the express purpose of presenting a paper to the conferenece on Designing for the Elderly, held in Nashville, Tennessee, November 1976, and organised by the American Institute of Architects and Center on Aging and Human Development. The visit has proved valuable for this study in a number of ways and has enlarged my understanding of the extent of the common problems facing our countries, consequent upon an absolute growth in numbers of old people and the relative proportion of the total population which they constitute.

Finally, a special word of thanks to both my secretary, Sue Clarke, who in addition to coping with all the work associated with being Departmental Secretary, has had to produce this report, and to Nicole Mainwaring who has been responsible for the graphics.

Edgar A. Rose
January 1978

NOTES

1. 'Housing the Elderly', Central Mortgage and Housing Corporation, Canada, 1975
2. 'The Sociological Imagination', Penguin, 1970
3. Ministry of Health Circular (HM 57), 86
4. 'Hanover Housing Association Study - Final Report', Mercer, D. and Muir, T., CURS, University of Birmingham, 1969
5. See, for example, an important speech by Dr. David Owen, the then Minister of State for Health, to the British Association for the Advancement of Science, 17th June, 1976
6. 'Public Planning: the intercorporate dimension', Friend, J.K., Power, J.M. and Yewlett, C.J., Tavistock, 1974
7. During the course of the study, the National Building Agency published a bibliography, and various other research studies were discovered at various stages of completion.

2 Summary and conclusions

INTRODUCTION

The primary objectives of the feasibility study were to appraise the:

(i)   design
(ii) location, and
(iii) management features

of 125 sheltered housing schemes built between 1967 and 1975, and to

(iv) assess the extent to which the needs of the elderly are satisified, and
(v)   to propose improvements for future developments including experimental features as set out in the terms of reference (Appendix IV).

The study comprised three stages:

Stage 1: The desk study of relevant literature and research. This allowed a series of perspectives to be drawn and a number of assumptions and working hypotheses, primarily concerned with the policy context were formulated. Other research findings in part provided the basis for the questions asked in the second stage warden survey.

Stage 2: The postal questionnaire survey of all wardens in 125 schemes. This sought to elicit the critical responses and identify problem areas that required more detailed examination.

Stage 3: The second personal interview and questionnaire survey. This consisted of a 50 per cent sample of the tenants in ten selected schemes (164 respondents).

The questions were concentrated on tenants' evaluations of six critical aspects identified by the warden questionnaire. In this chapter we briefly summarise and comment on the main points to emerge from the desk study; the state of research, the direction of development and research; some of the glaring gaps in current work. Having briefly summarised the results and analysis of the warden and tenant surveys, we go on to draw some conclusions and make a number of important recommendations and suggestions of relevance both to the Hanover Housing Association and others concerned with policy, design and management of homes for the aged.

RELEVANT RESEARCH

Research on sheltered housing is part of a wider spectrum which includes:

(i)   Aspects which are relevant to the design of housing in general
(ii)   Policy studies with regard to the aged in general.

The test of relevance so far as the Hanover Study is concerned remains research specifically related to sheltered housing though inevitably some relatively peripheral work was important enough to be included. The selected bibliography contains 122 items.

An evaluation may usefully focus on a 'core area' and the successive stages which categorise research in this field of study.

(i)   The introduction of the idea of sheltered housing was followed by research into the application of ergonomic principles to design in an attempt to identify where the needs of the elderly differed from those of others in the population. Much of this research and subsequent evaluation was promoted by, and carried out within, the then Ministry of Housing and Local Government (Hole, 1961; Hole and Allen, 1962; MHLG, 1957; MHLG, 1967; MHLG, 1966) and resulted in the publishing of design guidelines. Of particular note was Goldsmith's work on housing for the disabled. (Goldsmith, 1963)

(ii)   Following the completion of many schemes several evaluation studies were set up with a variety of aims and methodologies. The most notable were again

17

those carried out by and for government. Work which led to the redefinition of guidelines. (DOE, 1968; DOE, 1976; MHLG, 1966; MHLG, 1969) In addition, there was the work of Page and Muir for Hanover (Mercer and Muir, 1969; Page and Muir, 1971) and a large number of relatively small scale evaluation studies.

(iii)   In contrast several aspects of sheltered housing have received particular attention:
       alarm systems (Feeney, 1975 a & b)
       role of warden (Boldy, 1973 a & b)
       Outside the direct field of sheltered housing the work of Hillman on mobility of the elderly has considerable relevancy for locational aspects. (Hillman, 1973; Hillman, 1974)

(iv)   The many gaps in research are evident though some are the subject of current study, for example:
       (a)   Economic (cost) of different types of provision; sheltered housing compared with domiciliary care - an Essex County Council Study. (Wager, 1972)
       (b)   Behavioural research approaches to identification of needs compared with 'normal' population. Important research adopting this approach is being carried out by the Transport and Road Research Laboratory into mobility and location. (TRRL, 1974-76)
             As yet, other aspects of sheltered housing, e.g. behaviour/use of common facilities; social behaviour, etc. have not been investigated (except in so far as they are given considerable attention in this study.)
       (c)   Action research/experiments which promise much are conspicuous by their virtual absence.

Very few specifically research oriented sheltered housing schemes or specific features of schemes have been constructed. The importance of new design features and monitoring exercises has not been sufficiently realised yet. Isolated examples of such an approach do exist; for example,

18

a linked sheltered housing/residential home study; a meals service in one of Hanover's schemes (Bracknell) included in our study. More recently, the Beth Johnson Foundation (whose objective is action research for the elderly) has embarked on construction of a new scheme which will be monitored.

This brief summary indicates the need to systematically review progress in this field from several perspectives. Our overriding impression is that despite the wealth of experience and amount of building in this area, there has been inadequate systematisation of practice procedures whether related to design or management. Pragmatism reigns supreme and the different associations, for example, tend to go their own way. Although the fruits of shared experience are conspicuously absent, there are some examples of enterprise and initiative. Sheltered housing has avoided many of the pitfalls which have befallen standardised, mass produced, high rise public housing. The scale of schemes has remained human and environmentally satisfactory.

Nevertheless, it remains necessary to re-examine past practice and, without repeating work that has already been done, to focus upon the economic, behavioural and experimental aspects of designing for the aged. For reasons which have become obvious, experimental schemes which focus on improving heating and sound insulation rather than the problems of old people, per se have direct relevance and application as we become increasingly aware of the diminishing resources and escalating costs of fossil fuels.

THE WARDEN SURVEY (CHAPTER 3)

The questionnaire to the wardens of all Hanover schemes focussed on issues which reflected the emphasis devoted to them in the literature and were matters explicitly or implicitly referred to in the terms of reference. The Interim Report reproduces the summary tables on which Chapter 3 is based.

(i)   Postal questionnaires were sent to wardens in 125

19

schemes, 96.2 per cent of Hanover schemes completed up to September 1975. 105 were returned for analysis.

(ii)   A large majority of the schemes were single or double bedroom units, over a third had no communal facilities at all; only a small number of tenants were single males (5 per cent) and only 2.7 per cent of the tenants were chronically housebound.

(iii)   The questionnaires investigated specific aspects of the schemes as well as providing the opportunity for open-ended questions where wardens were invited to make additional comments.

(iv)   Dissatisfaction was expressed at the lack of provision of communal facilities, especially with the lack of a common room, although there was some variation in the attitudes of wardens without common rooms as to whether or not they would be a welcome addition.

(v)   The electric ceiling heating systems were found to be the least satisfactory with regard to effectiveness, ease of operation, etc. Electric ceiling heating was judged to be the most expensive.

(vi)   Internal sources of noise were judged to be a cause of annoyance by 28 per cent of the wardens. In cases where schemes were situated near to town centres or busy roads, external noise became a significant problem.

(vii)   The cost of bus services and their frequency was a more significant cause for dissatisfaction than the location of the scheme itself.

(viii)   There was dissatisfaction expressed by wardens of their dwellings more often when there was only one bedroom supplied than where there were two.(1) Privacy and storage facilities accounted for less dissatisfaction, and privacy was especially related to the existence of a separate entrance.

20

(ix) There was only contact between wardens in 44 per cent of the cases surveyed and some preference for a better network of informal contact was expressed.(2)

(x) The lack of external seating was mentioned by 27 per cent of wardens and outdoor drying areas were often insufficient in number. Gardening opportunities were seen as adequate by most wardens although inevitably problems arose where tenants could not continue to care for a plot. The privacy of the scheme was seen to be inadequate by 12 per cent of wardens and suggestions were made to better insulate the site from use by pedestrians and car owners among the public. Other external site features such as landscaping, paths and lighting were generally judged positively.

(xi) Looking at location, proximity to a chemist's shop was the most frequently mentioned problem, with distance to the town centre and post office mentioned next.

(xii) Almost a quarter of the wardens expressed the view that fire precautions were inadequate and lack of fire fighting equipment was perceived as the main problem.(3) The alarm call system was judged by some wardens as unsatisfactory because of unreliability and slow repair work, and also insufficient numbers of activation points in the flats.(4)

(xiii) Responses to open-ended questions complemented the specific questions. Communal facilities and the warden's dwelling were again the predominant features mentioned.

The six most important headings identified were:

(i)   Noise (airborne and structural)
(ii) Safety and fire hazard
(iii) Communal facilities
(iv) Location and accessibility

21

(v) Privacy of dwellings and of site
(vi) Heating type and cost.

Design and space requirements

Recent research has revealed confusion as to the role of wardens in sheltered housing schemes. Their role is perceived differently by the various groups involved. Nevertheless, although the role may lack definition it is increasingly recognised as important.

The wardens seek privacy for themselves and their families. There is an increasing amount of records to be filed, paper work to do, meetings with representatives of the social service, health visitors, and last but not least relatives of tenants.

THE TENANT SURVEY (CHAPTER 4)

The questionnaire to the tenants was concerned with responses that may be grouped under the six headings listed above. Appendix I provides twenty-five tables providing the summary data on which Chapter 4 is based.

General comments

Ten schemes were surveyed with half the tenants on each scheme being interviewed, making a total of 166 tenants. Schemes were located in the south west, north west and south of England and represented a variety of locations with regard to town centres, time of opening and types of heating systems installed.

80.5 per cent of the sample interviewed were single or widowed persons, which means that there were slightly fewer married couples in the selected schemes than is generally the case for Hanover. Average ages of tenants ranged from 70 to 77, but there was not a very close relationship between the age of the scheme and the age of the tenants (although of those schemes opened since 1973 there is none with anyone over 80) showing that Hanover have achieved an evenly distributed range of age levels in their schemes.

22

A total of 85.1 per cent of tenants said they were generally satisfied or very satisfied with their flats. Only 3 per cent expressed any appreciable degree of discontent. When asked for more specific 'likes' tenants most often referred to the pleasant view and satisfactory location of the scheme with respect to the town. Favourable comments about the compactness and ease of running of the flats were also very common.

Dissatisfaction was most frequently expressed with the heating, especially about its cost; this together with complaints about high rates or rents was a common theme. Problems relating to the design of windows were mentioned also.

Criticisms directed at specific schemes were the poor views from the 'rear end' of the Halifax scheme and the poor finish and construction of the Tewkesbury scheme.

Heating

Electric systems of heating scored particularly poorly in degree of satisfaction when tenants were asked specifically about it. Gas central heating on the other hand emerged as the most popular and effective method of heating, whereas electric storage and underfloor heating were not warm enough.

More tenants found it necessary to use additional forms of heating with electric systems, and in the case of ceiling heating 96 per cent used another form of heating, and 72 per cent did not use the system provided at all.

Electric systems cost more on average, although there were wide variations between individual users. Generally, those who believed that their heating bills were above average were correct. Additional remarks related to the expense of immersion heaters and the bulkiness of storage heaters. It should also be noted that satisfaction and praise were very common; many people remarking on their comfort and the convenience of their heating system. Heating bills were usually paid for quarterly. Payment was included in the rent in two schemes, an arrangement which appeared to be popular.

Noise

Using data from all schemes, only 24 per cent of tenants said they were bothered by noise. In the Tewkesbury scheme, located in the town centre, this rose to about 40 per cent. Although tenants could often hear neighbours' TV or plumbing, this did not usually bother them; it was unexpected noises from stairs, lifts and banging doors which caused most problems. External sources of noise, like heavy traffic often continuing at night, were more frequent where schemes were situated close to facilities like shops, but in no cases did there seem to be very serious problems.

Safety

97.5 per cent of tenants thought an alarm system was necessary but no one had found it necessary to use it more than five times in the past year. In fact, only 22 per cent of tenants had used the alarm at all. In three cases the alarm had not been effective and there was some concern expressed about the number of activation points and the ease with which the alarm cord could be mistaken for a light cord. Comments suggested that more frequent checking and better explanation of how to operate the alarm would be helpful.

The design of the flats was seen to be above average from the viewpoint of safety, although particular problems arose in some schemes - bathroom poles in Bracknell, high cupboards in Surbiton. Tenants' suggestions for design improvements show windows to be at the top of the list of priorities with cupboards and bathroom design next.

Communal facilities

Questions about communal facilities sought to investigate the use of and demand for such provision as well as the behavioural influences of such usage.

Washing machines were owned by 31 per cent of tenants and ownership was not affected by the existence of laundry facilities; similarly, as many people did their own washing as

24

those that used the scheme facilities where provided (Bracknell and Cirencester).

In these schemes some people did not use the laundry room because it was too crowded, suggesting that there is still some demand for such a facility which could be met by extra equipment. Tenants often had their washing done for them, or used the local launderette where available. There was a higher average proportion of tenants on the schemes with laundry facilities who said that these facilities were necessary. On other schemes there were large variations in people's preferences.

A higher proportion of tenants owned driers (54 per cent) than washing machines. Drying rooms were not as well used as laundry rooms. The distance to the drying facilities acted as a deterrent to use in some cases; as did the existence of a local launderette. However, where drying rooms did exist 60 per cent of tenants felt such a room was necessary; taking all schemes into account, 61 per cent thought such a room was necessary.

Six of the ten schemes had guest rooms. An average of 20 per cent of respondents had used the room in the last year, but only on two schemes (Cavendish Park and Cirencester) did the number of people using the guest room for visitors exceed the number using their own flats. In schemes without a guest room about 22 per cent of people had had someone to stay in their flats and 14 per cent had wanted someone to stay, but could not owing to lack of a guest room. Consideration of the number of people preferring to use their own flats even if a guest room was provided, and the predominance of short stay visits suggests that a multi-purpose unit would be more justified than a single purpose guest room. Schemes where a higher proportion of tenants originate locally have fewer overnight stays and the opposite applies where more tenants have moved into the area from outside.

Four schemes had a common room and the frequency of use varied, from less than once a week to every day. More activities were organised demonstrating the importance of the warden's role. High TV ownership means that there was little use for a TV lounge. Cheltenham's common room was

25

little used and the number of people saying a room was necessary was far lower than in the other three schemes. In schemes without a common room there was a varied response to the question of whether a room was necessary, ranging from 27 per cent in Cirencester to 85 per cent in Oldham. The actual use of common rooms was predominantly for organised events. This contrasts with the reasons given for wanting a common room which usually included the desirability of space for more informal social contacts and activities.

Although the number of tenants known to each other did not alter significantly with the existence or otherwise of a common room, the judgement of the adequacy of social contact did - 91 per cent of people in schemes with a common room thought there was sufficient contact as against 68 per cent in schemes where there was no room. Neither the number of outside activities nor the visiting of friends and relatives was closely related to provision of a common room, and so it appears that such provision does not replace tenants' outside activities. Casual factors were often difficult to establish. The most popular outside activities were church-going, closely followed by participation in pensioners' and social clubs.

Only one scheme (Cirencester) had a room officially described as a hobbies room, although tenants at Bracknell considered the common room to embody a hobbies room. At Cirencester the room was too small to be of use for hobbies and was used as a store room. At Bracknell about 60 per cent of tenants used the room over once a week and a vigorous tenants' committee organised regular evenings of social activity. In this same room lunches were served - one of the first of its kind built by Hanover, but there was only a small number of regular patrons, other tenants preferring to cook for themselves or make alternative arrangements rather than to be tied to a regular meal time.

Privacy

Asked whether schemes were private enough, too private or not private enough, 80 per cent of tenants thought they were private enough. At Bolton and Royton over 20 per cent of

26

tenants thought there was not enough privacy. In most cases the number of people mentioning children playing and people using the grounds as a short cut was related to assessments of privacy. But at Bracknell and Oldham some people noticed 'outsiders' in the grounds without finding this constituted a nuisance. In contrast, all tenants at the Royton scheme noticed children playing and people taking a short cut across their territory. An average of 25 per cent of tenants wanted to make the site more private by establishing some kind of boundary.

Location

Location presents complex issues of perception and interacting factors. The distance to a chemist and town centre appeared to be the critical factors. The selected schemes were various distances from their respective centres. But this distance was not consistently related to the degree of satisfaction expressed by tenants. The nearness of other shops or the existence of a good bus service compensated in some cases for the distance to the centre itself. There were six schemes which were more than a quarter of a mile from either post office or general store and respondents tended to judge these sites as less than very convenient.

Although closeness to the centre affected the amount of shopping done there, the notable exception was Bolton; there a direct, cheap and regular bus service enouraged 60 per cent of tenants to use the centre which was considered to be very conveniently located. By contrast, the Bracknell scheme had a far more expensive bus service, and was considered much less conveniently located not least because there were no alternative facilities readily accessible in the immediate vicinity. Tenants expressed a wish to be nearer the town centre in only four schemes; though in Bracknell this amounted to 41 per cent of the sample. With the exception of Bracknell, bus services were judged to be between convenient and very convenient in all schemes. Only 13 of the 164 people interviewed had cars - a total of almost 8 per cent.

The convenience of church and post office was clearly

27

related to their distances away. They were judged to be inconvenient if more than three quarters of a mile away.

Taking all the schemes together, problems with walking fell into three categories -traffic and difficulties crossing the roads, steep slopes and poor condition of pavements. In three schemes over half the respondents mentioned such problems - Cirencester (poor pavements), Oldham (heavy traffic) and Bracknell (no pavements and heavy traffic).

Responses to the question of missing facilities in the locality provoked positive replies from half the tenants of two schemes - Oldham and Bracknell; post office, chemist and fresh food shops are the most often mentioned.

DESIGN IMPROVEMENTS

It is not sufficient in our view to allocate a dwelling for the use of the warden which is identical to the tenants. Those wardens with two bedrooms expressed less dissatisfaction than those with only one . From our observations and the responses of wardens, themselves, it is clear that their space requirements need further study with a view to clearer design specification meeting criteria derived from the work they have to do and the need for privacy. Hanover has recognised the importance of this and they have now provided separate offices in ten schemes.

We recommend that normally wardens be provided with an office and a telephone; separate access other than from their dwelling should be provided, affording independent usage by a deputy warden. Adequate storage and a lock up garage are also essential.

Communal space

Communal facilities and their level of usage varies considerably within Hanover's schemes and the evidence suggests the need for more detailed study. Despite a large number of people using their own washing machine, laundry and drying rooms are well used. The proximity or otherwise of commercial launderettes is a relevant consideration.

28

Certainly the location of laundry and drying facilities is seen as of critical importance. Where schemes include a guest room, the level of usage hardly justifies its inclusion as a self-contained unit. There is scope for experiment here in providing multi-purpose space possibly with a linked free-standing shower unit appropriately located to serve a variety of uses. The provision of a common room which may be used for a variety of purposes including hobbies or for dining is accepted as conventional wisdom though practice varies considerably from scheme to scheme. In one scheme a room large enough to house all tenants was used only once a week. On the other hand the inability to divide a large space and the absence of satisfactory ventilation together conspired against the greater use of the space. Existing schemes may in many cases be improved by skilful adaptations. New projects need to include flexible and adaptable spaces which enable maximum use to be made of them. The location of such facilities is important. Respondents were sometimes discouraged by what they perceived to be too long a walk. In only one scheme was a dining room included. The level of usage was low and it seems that the desire for independence asserted itself more than in respect of any other common activity. People want to eat when they wish and evidently enjoy self-catering. Married couples especially who have always dined as a family are unwilling to change the habits of a life-time.

Noise

Using data from all schemes, one person in five said they suffered a degree of annoyance by noise. Tenants living on schemes located in a town centre (Tewkesbury) were disturbed by traffic noise. Although tenants agreed they could often hear neighbours' TV or plumbing, this normally was not considered a nuisance. Unexpected noises such as banging doors or from public stairs troubled people the most. It is possible that people who were exposed to external sources of noise like heavy traffic accepted that this was the price of living near the town centre and shops. The important conclusion is that neither external nor internal noise appears to be a serious problem. If more purpose designed or conversion schemes are to be built in or near town centres, then it will be necessary to consider ways of minimising the

29

impact of traffic noise. Reducing noise at source remains the most effective response.

Safety

The primary worry of some tenants concerned alarm systems and the number of activation points provided within the dwelling. There was a fear of falling some distance from the cord or button and being unable to reach it. The question of cost is obviously critical. Thr relatively low number of emergency calls registered in the schemes selected, and the high costs of such systems, suggests that it will be difficult to improve on present practice though specialised research in this field is taking place. The introduction in some schemes of an intercom system allowing two way conversation appears to have been very successful. (5) This system has presented some difficulty for deaf residents. Activation points must inevitably be limited, but on the other hand the warden can speak directly with tenants she considers may need assistance

Heating systems

The cost of heating was the most frequent and serious complaint of tenants. Although the costs of fuel have risen dramatically in the last few years, this does not entirely account for the concern. Dwellings in the UK remain for the most part single glazed and rely on natural ventilation. It is evident that these design standards are likely to be less acceptable to elderly people. Certainly, their ability to adapt to temperature change, to open and close windows, or to clean them, becomes more difficult with advancing years and infirmity of any kind. Various heating systems have been used in Hanover's schemes including electric ceiling heating which was so unpopular and expensive that 96 per cent of those with ceiling heating systems used supplementary heating and 72 per cent did not use the system at all. Electric storage and underfloor heating was also expensive and declared inadequate in cold weather. Those tenants with gas central heating were the most satisfied. In our view, double glazing will become relatively less costly as the cost of energy rises. Continental practice would overcome many of the problems alluded to.

The dwelling unit

The tenants find their homes generally very satisfactory. The most frequent criticism relates to the design of windows, difficulties in cleaning large expanses of glass, absence of transoms in some cases and opening lights in others. It is apparent that despite improvements in window design this is one general design feature that would benefit from further study and controlled experimental use of alternative designs. There were a number of detailed criticisms about the height and positioning of cupboards.

External areas

The tenants valued privacy highly and resented incursions into their territory by children and others on foot. They want their schemes shielded from general view and respond to a degree of physical separation, whether by difference of level or planting, between public and private areas. Generally, Hanover's schemes have responded to these views and generally landscaping, footpaths and lighting features are considered satisfactory. The opportunities for gardening are welcomed. Criticisms relate to small if important details like the provision of adequate garden seating and shielded drying areas. There are improvements and adaptations to existing schemes which could be carried out at relatively low cost whilst design criteria for new schemes could be formulated with greater precision.

LOCATIONAL REQUIREMENTS

Hanover's site requirements require a range of facilities to be normally within a quarter of a mile of a scheme and broadly speaking this requirement has been met in practice. Most tenants were able to reach all facilities and amenities they required on foot. The research was not designed to assess or measure trade offs between facilities though it is recognised that this is of considerable importance. (6)

What was evident was that shopping, the most frequent

activity requiring travel to and from the home, was well provided for. The elderly people clearly enjoyed the activity so that the journey to the town centre, not necessarily for essential shopping, was much appreciated. Many respondents liked to walk (where near enough) or take a bus to the centre simply to walk around and meet folk.

We are conscious of the diversity of environmental conditions, the complexity of attempting any definitive judgements as to location and the preferences of a group that, despite the term 'elderly', is far from homogeneous. Research effort is currently concentrating on the mobility of the elderly, their travel patterns, road safety, and use of facilities (shopping in particular). Further research is needed here with the emphasis increasingly directed towards problems of access to facilities rather than mobility as such.

It may be that the cost of providing new or extended services and facilities will become increasingly difficult in low density, peripheral areas so that questions of access and mobility will need to be related more closely to the locational requirements of a sheltered or any other form of housing scheme for the elderly.

Of particular importance would be knowledge of the cost of providing alternative forms of services, housing, facilities for the elderly, and knowledge of the cost in different parts of the city - where the density of existing settlement and ancillary facilities may be relatively compact and satisfactory compared with green field or edge of town sites.

We have tended to the view that whilst there is no ideal or optimal location which will satisfy all tenants at all times, it is possible to find out sufficient about social costs and personal preferences to formulate policy criteria which are more informed by facts than current practice.

MANAGERIAL FUNCTIONS

We have already emphasised the role and space requirements of the warden. The concept of a resident warden who is more than a landlady, but less than a nurse is relatively new. The

32

wardens pointed out that there was no organised contact or exchange of views between them (this is no longer the case). There was some informal and non-systematic contact in about 44 per cent of cases. A significant number of wardens wanted an improved management structure that would bridge this lack of communication and there may well be advantages in the idea of a National Association for Wardens which has been mooted by an Age Concern Working Party.

Our evidence also suggests an important role for wardens in advising prospective tenants and assisting them once they have arrived to settle in. It appears to be increasingly the case that elderly parents move home - sometimes long distances -to be near their children or other relatives. It is not satisfactory that all the decisions and arrangements pertaining to entry into a sheltered housing scheme are taken in their absence. The prospective tenant's relationship with the warden ought to be established before any decision is taken. In short, the expectations of any prospective tenants affect the subsequent degree of satisfaction experienced.

CONCLUSIONS

General policy

There is no doubt that the results of this study are encouraging and despite all the questions which have been raised by wardens and tenants alike, the vast majority of those living in the schemes examined enjoy their homes and display high levels of satisfaction with their environment and the facilities which are offered. In many ways the evidence suggests that this type of sheltered housing scheme provides a model which deserves to be more widely emulated as the need to provide more extensive provision of homes for the aged is realised. It is evident that such a view has considerable implications for social policy, resource allocation, and organisation.

Whilst this is not the place for a theoretical discussion of the limitations imposed by adopting attitudinal tests and relatively simple scaling techniques, the point needs to be noted if only because of the absence of longitudinal data and studies in this field, and the difficulty inherent in carrying out detailed observations over any useful period of time of the way space was used and people behaved.

What is important practically is that the schemes and the individual homes appeared to meet expectations of a group of individuals who applied for, and chose to live in this type of environment. It should be appreciated that there is self-selection in the sense that no one lives in a scheme who has not chosen to do so. The Association clearly understands the section of the public which it seeks to serve and has self-evidently prospered and been successful partly on that account. It has attempted to provide a 'code of practice' and the results generally suggest that it has been reasonably effective given the financial and institutional constraints. Within narrow limits there has been some experiment, but like the other sectors of the housing market, there has not been any bold innovation.

Our research confirms the general view that there are likely to be important payoffs from studying ways in which variety in sheltered housing is provided. For example, by the imaginative use and adaptation of existing stock which may well be better value for money than purpose built units in conditions of inflation, public expenditure restrictions and land shortage. There is no doubt that housing associations and often local authorities, searching for 'suitable' building sites have had no very explicit location policy. Land prices and shortages influenced the decision. The narrowest economic criteria prevailed. This is not so much a criticism as a recognition of the constraints which have existed. An explicit locational policy related to improvement of existing properties would have advantages for many old people who want to remain in the community and near their family.

Moreover, the outflow of population and jobs from middle and inner city areas is now recognised as a negative and potentially disastrous development. In the middle rings of our cities there is a relatively high density provision of building and appropriate range of ancillary facilities. There is an infrastructure which includes a familiar pattern and distribution of shops and public transport to name but two factors of obvious importance to the old, the infirm, children and those without cars.

Social expectations and professional judgements have changed and continue to change. Whilst this research has been underway, the Government's own proposals for future development have been set out in a consultative document. (7) More specifically, there has been increasing questioning of the quality or value, not to mention the cost of, institutionalised care. This suggests policy options which may offer an attractive, expanding and increasingly diverse role for housing associations such as Hanover. Government support for co-operative housing has also been forthcoming recently with the publication of the Report by the Campbell Committee. (8) What seems clear is that some of the assumptions which have underpinned work in this field will need to be revised. The primary objective for services used mainly by the elderly is to help them remain independent or relatively independent for as long as possible. This study focussed on those old people who can afford access to sheltered housing and are eligible to receive the support that an organisaton such as Hanover can provide. These people exercise choice wihin broad limits so that their preferences are useful indicators. Such evidence that we have underlines their desire for independence, to be near family and within reach of a wide range of facilities. In these circumstances, independence is highly valued provided that the appropriate support systems exist to give assistance and reassurance when required.

Experimental schemes

There are many proposals for experimental schemes which deserve most careful consideration by government and other agencies. Some are complex in that they go beyond physical design and require system design skills and the introduction of new social networks involving a variety of institutions including government. Others are relatively simple. What must be appreciated more clearly than hitherto are the institutional and financial constraints which exist, effectively preventing experiment and innovation. The Hanover Housing Association is only one of many agencies, governmental as well as voluntary, that would benefit from positive encouragement to experiment in one or more of the following:

(i)   Greater variations in dwelling sizes and methods of
        grouping dwellings within schemes; specifically, the
        introduction of specially designed bedsitters together
        with increased provision of shared facilities by groups
        and increased provision of communal facilities for
        the scheme as a whole.

(ii)   Greater variation in size of schemes and categories
        of old persons' dwellings. If additional facilities to
        serve the partially disabled and the sick are required
        within the scheme, then the optimum size may well
        be very different from those currently provided by
        Associations or the 'active elderly'.

(iii)   Taking advantage of air space in central areas or in
        district shopping centres of cities and towns. There
        may be the opportunity to take advantage of roof
        decks at first floor level, above shopping and
        commercial activities which only require low level
        accommodation. Many private developers may be
        willing to incorporate such facilities as part of a
        negotiated development with the local planning
        authority, especially where the land is owned by the
        community.

(iv)   Improved thermal and acoustic insulation; integrated
        technical systems designed to conserve energy.

(v)   Conversion of existing accommodation of varying
        characteristics on appropriately located sites in the
        arcadian middle ring of cities.

(vi)   More controlled experiments in the provision and use
        of communal space, both inside and outside the
        building.

(vii)   Experimental design of wardens' accommodation and
        office. It may be related to the provision of a flat

and shower unit suitable for those disabled and temporarily ill.

(viii) Relationships between sheltered housing and other service and care facilities on the same or nearby sites.

(ix) Relationships between sheltered housing and tailored adaptations of normal (family-type) houses to suit the partially disabled or the less mobile.

(x) The provision of service flats in central areas together with combined support facilities.

It will be evident from the foregoing that the study has persuaded us of the value of building schemes which explore overall concepts of an old person's dwelling and its relationship not simply to family housing and social amenities, but to the housing group of which it forms a part. Some of these ideas will require further study before a sound and cost-effective brief emerges.

The need for closer collaboration with other agencies and Associations in promoting such so-called experimental schemes is a pre-condition for success if any new initiatives are to be tried. It is becoming increasingly important to examine within the planning process, the social if not the physical impact of growing concentrations of old people and old people's housing schemes on existing towns and neighbourhoods. Surveys will have to give greater attention not only to current facilities and services, but to the likely future demand for housing by the elderly and its probable impact on community resources.

The feasibility of Hanover Housing Association embarking on any of the experimental schemes is clearly a matter primarily for the Association. Some of the ideas advanced could be interpreted modestly and relatively small scale departures from existing norms could be pursued within a philosophy that accepted that gains in one area would be traded off for losses in another. A major difficulty may well be that experimental schemes are refused financial support because they depart from established norms.

However, it must be stated that the value of experimental policies, whether relevant to design, location or management, can only be determined by establishing an effective monitoring or review function within this field of work. Research and development monitoring and policy review needs to be better co-ordinated within the voluntary sector, so that at the least, longitudinal surveys that include behavioural response are undertaken. Without this, progress is likely to be slow and the more fundamental aspects risk being lost sight of. As we said in our initial working note:

'The feasibility study should concentrate in part at least on the hypothesis that housing design for the elderly might be improved in a practical fashion by increasing the understanding of the behaviour of elderly people and an understanding of their preferences'.

Further research

The quality and efficiency of administrative services within a project or related to a number of projects is related to size. Some fragmentary evidence suggests that more facilities can be provided and warden and other support used   more effectively in schemes of between 100 and 150 units. Whilst the dangers of over large schemes must be avoided, it is necessary to promote much more rigorous studies of the costs of providing various units of and variations in accommodation and the economies of scale which may accrue from increasing size. A fundamental and relatively straightforward study would be to set out the relative costs associated with a number of alternative schemes so that the options open to policy makers and designers alike are understood in terms of resources and expressed preferences from the brief stage onwards. Such information has been systematised for more complex buildings and could be collated for the range of facilities being discussed here.

It has been said that the trick of discovering which set of attributes prospective purchasers would value, and of discovering a product configuration capable of embodying them at the right price is the exercise known as designing. (9) It is the subtle ratio between specification and performance and price that is of critical importance to government, consumer and designer. Where social budgets are fixed or incomes are limited, cost effectiveness becomes the sine qua non of good design. The designers will be seeking improvements at the margin - which improvements the consumer will feel are worth paying extra for.

With these considerations in mind, we suggest just three of a number of topics which require much more detailed study than hitherto. The first is the re-examination of conversion as a means of improving the supply of sheltered housing. The demand for sheltered housing is likely to increase over the next two decades as the number of retired persons increases; and also as the concept of warden supervised housing becomes more widespread and known. The second is the provision of communal facilities in sheltered housing. The provision of communal facilities in sheltered housing is not based on a sufficiently sound set of criteria. The third is the location of sheltered housing. As previously stated, current research is concentrating on the mobility of the elderly, their travel patterns and use of facilities (shopping in particular). Other aspects relevant to location are also under investigation, e.g. safety of the elderly from traffic. However, this information has not yet been drawn together and related to the locational requirements of a sheltered housing (or the type of housing for the elderly) scheme.

It has been correctly suggested that the differences in institutions and administrative practice between the UK and, for example, the US or other countries in Europe needs to be explicitly recognised in any cross-cultural comparisons. The brief references to Dutch and American policy and practice illustrate the potential value of a comparative study of policy and practice in housing for the aged within the European Community and the United States. The first stage of such a study would no doubt examine the standards adopted within each country and the relative importance attached to various categories of dwellings and relevant regulations.

Design standards and terms of reference

A specific review of Hanover's Design Brief has not been undertaken as an explicit part of this study. It is understood that it is constantly reviewed and systematised and will have regard to this study. Such design manuals and codes of practice cannot guarantee good design, but they can indicate clearly what is expected by the client.

Two further recommendations of considerable importance, which relate directly to questions raised in the terms of reference, have wider application.

(i)   There is little evidence of vandalism, but this largely reflects the location and socio-economic characteristics of the neighbourhoods in which the schemes were located. There is little doubt that design will have to take into account both security of persons and property in sensitive locations.

(ii)   The private telephone is widely used and is an invaluable lifeline for old people. Nevertheless, the evidence of growing financial problems of those on fixed incomes in paying rent and heating bills suggests that the provision of a public telephone in every scheme should be normal practice. If the principle of sheltered housing is extended to a wider section of the community and current policy directions suggest this to be the case, then either a group of dwelling units share a hall telephone, reducing the number provided overall, or a public telephone is installed using standard procedure.

In conclusion, it only remains to emphasise that further developments in housing design and physical research in these areas will yield important spin-off which in many cases will improve physical performance of sheltered housing.

NOTES

1. Hanover has provided second bedrooms in all wardens' dwellings since 1976; they are now provided as self-contained units, with separate entrances.
2. Annual meetings of Hanover's wardens have been held on a regional basis since 1976.
3. Fire precautions in all Hanover schemes are obviously in accordance with fire officers' requirements; such requirements vary. Since the warden postal questionnaire was sent out in February 1976, the fire officer has visited every Hanover scheme to meet both warden and tenants. The Association in their fourteenth annual report has intimated that it would welcome an independent review of the fire precaution requirements.
4. All schemes since 1976 have incorporated standard speech-call systems as standard practice; a continuous programme of upgrading of older systems is underway.
5. Now standard practice.
6. For example, specific facilities which tenants would be prepared to give up in exchange for other facilities - higher levels of thermal comfort in exchange for smaller dwellings.
7. 'Priorities for Health and Personal Services in England', 1976
8. Final Report of the Working Party on Housing Co-operatives, DOE, HMSO, 1975
9. Archer, L.B., "Design", Journal of the Royal Society of Arts, August 1976

3 The warden survey

INTRODUCTION

The response of the wardens of all schemes built by Hanover to the postal questionnaire indicated a number of issues which were considered important. The results of this initial survey were presented in the form of an Interim Report to Hanover's Management Committee and this chapter draws heavily upon that Report. The tenant survey which followed, reflected in part the wardens' perceptions of what were the key issues. The design and content of the questionnaire to the tenants was influenced therefore, by the results gained from the warden survey. The analysis of the tenants' replies indicated that many of the problems identified by the wardens were similarly regarded by other residents (see Appendix III, the Questionnaires).

As the research progressed and our knowledge grew firstly from the results of the desk study, secondly from the tenants themselves, and thirdly from discussions with Hanover's officers and others, the tentative formulations which were made in the Interim Report, appeared increasingly inadequate.

This chapter, therefore, seeks to summarise the essential points to emerge in that Report without indulging in needless repetition. The detailed tables which it contained are not reproduced here. The wardens' comments are reassessed and evaluated in the context of the tenants' subsequent responses. The conclusions suggest further research which is both feasible and necessary.

THE SURVEY

Objectives

The results of the literature search indicated the general need for and desirability of selecting a small number of issues for further study. Nevertheless, it was considered necessary to establish whether such issues were important or in need of further study in the context of Hanover schemes. Because the number of sheltered housing schemes has grown considerably since the initial study commissioned by Hanover (Page and Muir, 1968), it was decided in the first instance to contact the wardens of all the schemes. The questionnaire was designed to be as simple and as wide-ranging as possible. Apart from some initial profile data on the schemes, the wardens were asked to evaluate particular characteristics of their schemes. In addition, a number of open-ended questions were included to enable wardens to comment on aspects not necessarily covered in the previous, structured questions.

Sample size and response

Accordingly, postal questionnaires were sent out to the wardens of 125 schemes, for which addresses were available. This represents 96.2 per cent of the Hanover schemes completed up to September 1975. A total of 105 usable replies were received, a response rate of 84 per cent. A further 6 per cent of the questionnaires were returned unanswered for various reasons. All the information from the warden questionnaires was coded for ease of handling, although no computer analysis was undertaken. A preliminary analysis of the first 80 questionnaires received by the middle of March 1976 was used in the design of the second questionnaire.

A profile of Hanover schemes

The basic characteristics of the completed sample of schemes are given in Table 1 of Appendix 3, Interim Report. The salient points are as follows:

(i)   The majority (92 per cent) of the units in the sampled schemes were either single or double bedroom units. Only 5.6 per cent of the units had two bedrooms, and 2.4 per cent were bedsitters.

(ii)   Over a third (37 per cent) of the schemes had no communal facilities at all. The most frequently provided facility was a guest room, which was present in 56 per cent of the sampled schemes. Only 11 per cent of schemes had a common room, guest room and a laundry or drying room together.

(iii)   Just over a quarter (27 per cent) of the tenants of the sample schemes were male, of which the majority were married, 5 per cent of the tenants were single males.

(iv)   A total of 97 persons (2.7 per cent of the tenants) in the sampled schemes were chronically housebound, these persons living in 44 of the 105 schemes (including one scheme specially designed for the disabled housing 18 housebound persons).

(v)   A total of 88 persons (2.5 per cent) spread over 43 schemes were wanting to leave their schemes. In one scheme those wanting to leave formed 22 per cent of the number of tenants on that scheme.

Wardens were specifically asked in the postal questionnaire how many, if any, tenants wished to leave the schemes. They were not asked the reasons, although space was provided for comments on all the questions - two wardens commented on tenants wishing to move; two were waiting to be moved to another scheme nearer relatives and another was 'awaiting an exchange opportunity'. However, the total of 88 persons wishing to move must be put into perspective:

(i)   Those 88 lived on only 43 of the 125 schemes, i.e. on 82 schemes the wardens knew of no one wishing to leave.

(ii)   Account must be taken of what the expected turnover rate would be (excluding death which is the main cause of vacancies on schemes). Evidence from a study of schemes in Devon suggested that 3.5 per cent of tenants would change in a year, i.e. about 125 per year from the number of tenants in the schemes surveyed, which included deaths. This finding indicates that the total of 88 is not unreasonable.

(iii)   Of those tenants wishing to leave, 26 came from five particular schemes (Lowestoft III, Welwyn, Dewsbury, Wilstead, Scunthorpe) although the wardens' comments do not suggest the reasons for this concentration. In addition, 'several' were said to want to leave Bar Hill.

(iv) It is important to realise that the question was asked of wardens and not of the tenants themselves, i.e. the warden may not know of tenants' plans, or be translating just occasional gossip into firm plans. In either case the figure of 88 must be treated with care.

ANALYSIS OF WARDENS' RESPONSES

Evaluative questions

The major part of the questionnaire was taken up with evaluative questions of fifty one specific aspects of sheltered housing. In each case the warden was requested to give that aspect a score of 1 – Unsatisfactory; 2 - Indifferent; 3 - Satisfactory. In some cases additional factual information was requested, and space was left for the wardens to add their own comments. The analysis identified and ranked specific aspects on the basis of the importance of the issues as measured from the wardens' responses. Importance in this context refers to the degree of dissatisfaction with a particular feature. This has been measured in two ways; firstly, by the percentage of responses in the lowest category (i.e., 1 - Unsatisfactory) and secondly, by the median score given to that feature. Table 2 in Appendix 3 of the Interim Report measures for each feature ordered according to the median score. The most important issues are discussed under appropriate headings below. Use is made both of the additional factual information obtained, and of the comments made by wardens. The responses to the open-ended questions about the schemes are considered subsequently.

Communal facilities

57 per cent of the wardens (excluding the 36 wardens who did not respond to the question) evaluated their communal

45

facilities as unsatisfactory. Most of those wardens who did not respond did so because they had no communal facilities (especially no common room) and hence presumably felt that the question did not apply. Table 3 (Interim Report) shows the wardens' evaluations cross tabulated against the presence of communal facilities. It is apparent that the evaluations are closely related to the existence of a common room, rather than the other facilities. Seventeen out of the eighteen wardens on schemes including a common room said that their communal facilities were satisfactory; 39 of the remaining wardens said that they were unsatisfactory (a further 35 did not respond). Wardens' opinions on the necessity, or otherwise of these communal facilities was clearly divided, and probably depended not only on the characters of the wardens and of the tenants, but also on the locations of the schemes with respect to local facilities and services.

Heating

The second most unsatisfactory aspect according to the wardens' evaluations was the cost of heating in the schemes. This finding is subject to the major qualification that by the time of the survey, escalation in heating costs and its implications for the elderly had become a major national issue.(1)

The main interest in this survey is the comparison between different types of heating (Tables 4 and 5 Interim Report). The first table shows the wardens' general evaluation of the heating (i.e. its effectiveness, ease of operation, etc.). Of the three most frequently installed heating systems, two (gas warm air and electric ceiling heating) were said to be unsatisfactory or of indifferent quality by about one third of the wardens. A fifth of the wardens were dissatisfied with or unenthusiastic about the third system - electric storage heating - which was the most frequently used system. The dissatisfaction with electric ceiling heating is reflected in the fact that three wardens mentioned it specifically as something they would leave out of future schemes (Table 12, Interim Report).

When the heating costs are considered (Table 5, Interim

46

Report) it is electric storage heating which is the system with the largest proportion of wardens saying the cost is unsatisfactory (both electric warm air and gas-fired central heating also have high proportions scoring 'unsatisfactory' but the number of schemes with these heating systems is too small to make any more general conclusions).

The cost of heating is clearly a critical issue and the perceived cost is not only related to the actual cost of the heating, but also to the effectiveness of the heating system and to the method of charging for the heating. These aspects were followed up in the tenants' survey.

Noise

Three questions were included on noise: insulation from internal and external noise and the external level of noise. It was the insulation against internal noise which was evaluated as being the most unsatisfactory (28 per cent of the wardens said it was unsatisfactory), followed by the insulation from external noise (17 per cent said this was unsatisfactory). No additional information was requested from the wardens, but their additional comments suggest that noise from the flat above is the most common problem, followed by noise through the walls. Noise from television (particularly belonging to slightly deaf tenants) and telephones was mentioned most, though warm air heating systems evidently gave rise to annoyance. The main problem of external noise arose from schemes located near town centres or on busy or narrow roads. In two cases a nearby railway was the source, and in another it was schoolchildren. It was thought that tenants' reactions to noise were likely to be very varied and dependent upon a number of features and so this issue was also followed up in the tenant survey.

Bus service

33 per cent of the wardens felt that the bus service near the schemes was unsatisfactory. However, it is clear from an analysis of the comments the wardens made that in only one or two cases is this because of the scheme's location (e.g. 'no bus service', 'bus service across busy road'). By far the most critical factor was the cost of the bus trip which ranged from

47

free travel to about 60p return to the local centre.

The second factor was the level of service, frequency and times of operation. Some schemes had no evening or Sunday services. The use of bus services by tenants was subsequently investigated in the tenant survey and related to other locational factors.

Warden's dwelling

As the questionnaire was directed at wardens, it was anticipated that features of the scheme connected with the wardens and their duties would arouse more comment than many of the other aspects. To some extent this was borne out by the analysis. While wardens expressed little dissatisfaction with their duties and contacts with Hanover headquarters or tenants, a number of them found their own dwellings unsatisfactory in certain respects. Some criticism was expressed with accommodation, especially relating to privacy and storage facilities by 27 per cent, 17 per cent and 19 per cent of wardens respectively. In addition, 17 per cent of wardens were dissatisfied with the contacts they had with other wardens.

By cross-tabulating the evaluations of the warden's dwelling against the number of bedrooms the warden has, and against whether the warden has a separate entrance or a structurally separate dwelling from the tenants, it is evident that the number of bedrooms and degree of privacy may be closely related to the degree of satisfaction expressed with the dwelling. Of those wardens with only one bedroom, 21 per cent said that their dwelling was unsatisfactory. It is necessary to add that whilst a two bedroomed dwelling for the warden is a Hanover design requirement, 67 per cent of the sampled schemes nevertheless had only one bedroom warden accommodation.

The evaluations of the warden's privacy was cross-tabulated with whether the warden has a separate entrance, a structurally separate dwelling and an office. All three factors affect the evaluation of privacy. Between 28 per cent and 31 per cent of the wardens without separate entrances or dwellings or an office were dissatisfied with the

48

degree of privacy afforded, compared with between none and 18 per cent of the wardens living in dwellings possessing these attributes who also expressed dissatisfaction at lack of privacy. The strong desire for a separate, two bedroom dwelling with some place (e.g. office) where tenants may be received without any intrusion into the warden's own home is reflected also in the response to the open questions (Tables 10-14, Interim Report).

The other aspect of the wardens' evaluations which deserves mention is the felt need for informal contacts between wardens, themselves. 44 per cent of the wardens had no contact with any other wardens, and of those who responded with an evaluation as well (14 wardens), 9 were dissatisfied with this lack of contact.

From the additional comments made by the wardens, it is apparent that in many cases the opportunity to telephone a warden one knows and discuss problems informally is very important. Wardens who are new, or who live in schemes which are located in relative isolation from others may not be able to do this, simply because no initial personal contact has been made.

The establishment of information networks, formal and informal, may deserve further consideration.

External features: the site

A number of aspects of external site layout and design deserve mention. No additional profile information was gathered on this aspect, so the discussion is based to a large extent on the additional comments made by wardens.

Outdoor seating 27 per cent of wardens said that the outdoor seating was unsatisfactory. In most cases, this appeared to be either because no seating was provided, or there was no suitable or available space in which to put seating. In one case, the warden felt that additional seats would be appreciated. However, there is no evidence from the wardens' comments as to the likely use of such seating if it were provided. Like the opportunities for gardening (see below) the utilisation of facilities is dependent upon the behaviour or desired behaviour of the tenants, and this may vary widely from scheme to scheme. Nevertheless, generalisations may be made. It is reasonable to suggest that where it is possible to have the benefit of a view and be sheltered from the wind, there arguably is a suitable spot for outdoor seating. The solution which would appear appropriate in existing schemes would be to respond to individual requests for the provision of seating, possibly after some experiments with portable seating to establish preferred locations.

Clothes drying areas 18 per cent of the wardens felt that this provision for clothes drying was unsatisfactory in some way. In all but one case the dissatisfaction came from the inadequate size of the drying area or the numbers of rotary driers provided. Comments such as, "It's O.K. as long as too many tenants don't wash on the same day" were common. In one case, it was the location of the drying areas (too near the flats) which appeared to be the problem.

Gardening opportunities 63 per cent of the schemes had some kind of gardening opportunities for the tenants; and over three-quarters of these wardens who also gave a score to this question said that this was satisfactory (Table 8). Most of the wardens of schemes where gardening opportunities were not available did not say whether they felt that this was a satisfactory or an unsatisfactory state of affairs.

Additional comments by the wardens tended to be negative ones; "tenants show no interest in gardening" or "tenants don't look after them". Some wardens noted that their tenants took great pride in their plots. A couple of wardens mentioned the desirability of having raised gardens or containers to avoid the tenants having to stoop. As with the question of seating, a flexible approach appears necessary, with space being provided in the grounds if and when necessary. Schemes in which each tenant had a garden, inevitably had problems of maintenance, where the tenants no longer wished or were not able to cultivate their plots.

Privacy of scheme 12 per cent of wardens felt that the privacy of the scheme from surrounding areas was unsatisfactory, and 8 per cent that the security was unsatisfactory. The additional comments made (see particularly the open responses in Tables 11 and 14 (Interim Report)) suggest, as might be expected, that schemes with 'open plan' layout adjoining other residential areas or alongside rights of way had the greatest problems. In addition, the use by non-residents of the open parking areas was a source of nuisance on a number of schemes.

The most frequently suggested solution to the problem was to make some boundary (whether a physical or nominal boundary) around the scheme, and to restrict access by road or footpath into the scheme to tenants only in some way.

Other external site aspects Four other aspects of the site received little adverse comment from the wardens: the car parking, paths, lighting, and landscaping. These four aspects only appeared to be problems on particular schemes where, for example, sloping paths present hazards in icy weather, or where paths were inadequately lit at night. The appearance of the scheme was only referred to in two contexts: firstly, the state in which it was left by the contractors after construction, and secondly, the amount of maintenance required. The large areas of grass involved in some open plan sites, together with the problems of visual intrusion, led several wardens to suggest that open planning was unsuitable.

As far as car parking is concerned, it appeared that there was a general feeling that the space provided was often too large (hence inviting use by outsiders) and that more garages could replace some of this car parking area. The demand for car parking obviously varied greatly from scheme to scheme, and a minority of wardens felt that they had too many garages.

Location

Of all the facilities mentioned in the wardens' questionnaire, the location with respect to a chemist's shop was stated to be unsatisfactory in the most cases (27 per cent of schemes). Table 9 shows the percentage of wardens in each evaluation category for all the facilities. Alongside the percentage is the mean distance that the schemes were stated to be from the relevant facilities (wardens' estimates). In the case of the chemist the mean distance to a chemist's shop for the 23

51

schemes in the unsatisfactory category was 1.7 miles, and the overall mean for all schemes for which estimates were given was 0.8 miles.

The convenience to the town centre was the second most unsatisfactory aspect with 16 per cent unsatisfactory (mean distance 2.3 miles), followed by the convenience to a post office (13 per cent unsatisfactory; mean distance 0.9 miles).

It is clear from a consideration of the mean distances even within the satisfactory category, that not many schemes fulfil the Hanover site location requirements of 'normally within $\frac{1}{4}$ mile of shops, a regular bus route, post office, church and a pub'.

Although this requirement may be unnecessarily strict (and the evidence is that it is not) there were some schemes which were obviously poorly located with respect to facilities -there were cases of schemes being two, five and six miles from a chemist. Although the specifications in Hanover's site requirements do not include the 'desirable' distance of a chemist, this is one of the facilities which might usefully be included in the list, a conclusion which was given further support from the tenant survey.

An important consideration here is not only distance to a shop, but also the type of shop and even perhaps prices and selection of goods. This is the case at Bar Hill where a shopping precinct stands very close to the scheme and includes post office, bank, TV shop, DIY shop, chemist (no pharmacy) and a fish and chip shop, but where it is necessary to travel five miles to Cambridge for general provisions and fresh food.

The location of the schemes with respect to these, and other facilities (including bus services) may be critical to the life the tenants can lead, and to the degree of independence they can retain. This topic was investigated further in the tenants' questionnaire.(2)

Safety

Fire precautions Almost a quarter of the wardens (22.5 per

cent) said that fire safety was unsatisfactory. This was a surprising result because fire safety was not expected to be a critical issue. Analysis of the wardens' comments shows that in three-quarters of the cases the lack of fire fighting equipment was stated to be the problem. However, three other matters were also mentioned: the lack of alternative (fire) exits (or inability to open doors in an emergency); the irregular testing of existing equipment; and finally, on one scheme the warden noted that "No fire precautions recommended by the fire service had been applied".

This is a serious issue about which more information and consultation with fire authorities is required. Wardens may need informing as to the fire prevention features which are incorporated into schemes, but which they are not aware of. Consideration should perhaps be given to the need for some formal procedures involving both wardens and tenants as well as fire authorities. It was not felt possible to take this issue further in this study. The perceived inadequacy of fire safety provision was reported fully in the Interim Report and it is clearly a matter of critical importance for tenants and wardens alike to be reassured that there is no real cause for disquiet and that all fire precaution procedures are complied with.

Alarm systems 14 per cent of wardens were dissatisfied with the alarm call system. It has not been possible to relate these evaluations to the different types of system because of the often inadequate descriptions received from the wardens. The first was the unreliability of the system and the inability to get repairs done quickly. The second was the unsuitable positioning of some of the alarm cords or buttons, sometimes resulting in accidental operation or being unable to reach the alarm in a real emergency. This is a common problem, particularly when tenants' furniture is arranged in an unconventional position.

Open-ended questions

The responses to the five open-ended questions at the end of the questionnaire have been summarised under the following heads:
(i)   Internal design features

(ii)   External features
(iii)   Location
(iv)   Management
(including aspects of the wardens' dwellings, roles, etc.).

The responses to each of the five questions are listed in Tables 10-14 (Interim Report). Little further comment is required, because most of the issues have already been discussed. The following issues were mentioned by ten or more wardens:

The good location of the scheme for shops, services, etc.
The lack of a common room.
The need for a common room on new schemes.
The need for a laundry room (with washing machines) on new schemes.

It will be seen that both wardens' and communal facilities rank high on the list of problems and suggested improvements. These unsolicited responses reinforce the previous conclusions drawn from the questionnaire and elsewhere. Other matters which have not been dealt with, but which were mentioned by one or more wardens are: provision of a coin phone box for the schemes; ventilation problems; the pleasant setting of some schemes, and the possibility of providing showers in addition to baths.

INTERIM CONCLUSIONS

The aim of the wardens' questionnaire was to identify, and put in perspective, the important issues relating to Hanover schemes which could then be followed up in a survey of tenants. To some extent, therefore, the conclusions are illustrated by the tenants' questionnaire (Appendix III) and the issues it dealt with are discussed in Chapter 4.

Some important aspects have, however, not been included in the questionnaire, and these relate largely to the wardens and their accommodation. From the evidence of the survey it is clear that many wardens do not enjoy the privacy which they evidently need, nor do many have adequate facilities (in terms of office space or storage) to carry out their jobs efficiently without excessive intrusion into their own family lives. In addition, the practice of allotting the warden a dwelling which, in terms of size and design, is identical to the tenants' does not appear to be satisfactory. It is desirable that more emphasis should be placed in the Architectural Design Requirements on the needs and specifications of the warden's dwelling.

The need for office space does not have to involve a physically separate area; it is functional separation rather than physical which is required to ensure greater privacy for the warden and her family, and there is little ingenuity required to install an alarm system which can be switched over to ring in different locations, like the office itself or a deputy's flat. In several cases this arrangement has already been adopted by Hanover where wardens' office areas have been provided.

Another important issue which is not taken further is that of fire safety. The evidence suggests that there is real concern on the part of wardens. Our study suggests that it is essential to allay fears of tenants and wardens alike, however misplaced and unfounded they may be. The tenant survey, although not focussing directly on this issue, revealed some concern by tenants about apparent lack of fire fighting equipment, or clearly indicated fire exits in flats. However, in addition interviewers' remarks showed that in some cases fire fighting equipment was not clearly visible. Apart from the question of any purely physical design changes which are often very expensive and vary considerably from scheme to scheme and area to area, tenants could be made more aware of fire prevention methods and fire fighting equipment installed. The tenant survey suggests a potential risk results from use of heating either to dry clothes or warm bathrooms. This is discussed further in Chapter 4. Although it will never be possible to eliminate this danger altogether, the risk could be minimised by more systematic explanation of fire hazards.

It is likely that part of the problem remains poor communications between the relevant parties. If this is so then a first step could be taken without much cost. Clearly, further study of this problem is necessary and would involve fire authorities and wardens initially.

NOTES

1. By the time of drafting the Final Report in December 1976, the problem of high energy costs had begun to affect the building industry in many different ways. The ramifications of the problem were better appreciated and policies were under review. See, for example, "Solar Houses for the Elderly", RIBAJ, November 1976, which discusses construction due to begin on a prototype group of solar houses for the elderly at Bebington, Merseyside

2. One in three pensioners have difficulty in walking and one in three have difficulty in using public transport. See, 'Transport Realities and Planning Policy' by Hillman, Henderson and Whalley, PEP, December 1976. Especially, personal interview travel survey of pensioners in a wide area beyond the boundaries of Greater London.

4 The tenant survey

INTRODUCTION

The tenant survey was designed with the aim of exploring further the six issues which had been identified as critical from the first (warden) survey stage. The objective was in each case to specify more clearly the nature of the problem (i.e. the reasons for the wardens evaluating them as problem issues) and hence to be in a position to suggest design or procedural improvements.

The tenant questionnaire (see Appendix III) concentrated on the six issues, though tenants were also given the opportunity to express opinions about particular design features, or the scheme in general. A draft questionnaire was produced initially and after consultations with colleagues and officers of Hanover Housing Association, was amended and used in a small number of pilot interviews carried out with the tenants at the Hanover scheme at Tamworth. It was decided that the amount of profile data collected from the tenants should be minimal and restricted to age, sex, marital status and whether the respondents were ambulant or not.

This chapter, therefore, reports the results of the survey in some detail and needs to be read in conjunction with the appropriate tables referred to in the text and grouped in Appendix I.

THE SURVEY

Objectives

The objective of the tenant survey was primarily to find out what tenants thought of the schemes in which they lived and to ascertain how far the wardens had identified the problems which they perceived as important. A secondary objective was to ascertain whether any of the problems were related to design practices that had been discontinued or introduced by

Hanover over the years. Throughout this work we have been conscious of the difficulties, within the means and time available to us, of saying anything valuable which relates to the problems of ageing itself or indeed the problem of designing for a population in any scheme as it ages. This is in essence both a behavioural problem and a problem of adopting a design philosophy which allows for adaptability and flexibility in the use of space and the provision over time of facilities which may be needed. In short, we hypothesised not only the need for longitudinal studies of the kind briefly indicated here, but the need for controlled building design experiments, associated with much closer managerial links between Hanover and its wardens.

Above all, although the schemes are relatively small in size, very small compared with some schemes that were visited in the States, it was considered important to recognise the principle that the tenants themselves, as building users, could not only indicate their preferences, but also play a positive role in identifying both design and management improvements. What we could not do in this study was put a price on their preferences and indicate what they might be prepared to trade-off to secure a particular improvement. Nevertheless, we are conscious that in times of economic stringency such exercises will become more and more essential. Design, good design, will have to become more cost-effective. We think that this is certainly the view of tenants in relation to their heating bills, for example.

Criteria for selection of schemes and sample size

It was decided to carry out a detailed field survey of ten schemes and to interview tenants in half the units of the schemes. With an average of thirty units per scheme this gave an estimated sample size of 150 interviews. The schemes were chosen in accordance with the following criteria:

(i)   They had to be accessible to the interviewers. For this reason three areal groupings of schemes were first identified: the south west (Cheltenham) area, the north west (Lancashire/Pennines) area, and the Home Counties west of London.

58

(ii)   The schemes had to have a range of communal facilities.

(iii) The schemes had to have a range of different heating schemes.

(iv)   The schemes had preferably to have different locations with respect to town centres.

(v)   The schemes had to have a range of opening dates, in order to test whether the age of the schemes was of any significance.

A short list of twelve schemes was drawn up, from which, with the help of the officers of Hanover, the ten schemes were chosen. The basic characteristics of the ten schemes are summarised in Table 1. The total number of units on these schemes is 332, which produced a sample of 166 tenants.

Interviewing procedures

The personal interviews were carried out by postgraduate students from the Department of Architectural, Planning and Urban Studies in the University of Aston. The interviewers were briefed on the aims of the tenant survey, and on the findings of the warden survey, before they embarked on the field work. In addition to the actual interviewing, which took on average one hour per tenant, the interviewers were asked to write a brief factual description of the scheme and were invited to record their own impressions together with any comments made by the wardens.

Characteristics of tenants interviewed   A total of 164 interviews out of a possible 166 were successfully completed, representing a little less than one interview in every other dwelling unit in the ten schemes (49.4 per cent of units). Table 2 lists the number of interviews carried out for each scheme; 40.9 per cent of the total number of tenants on the schemes were interviewed.

The sample interviewed is slightly biassed towards single and female tenants, although the differences between the proportions on the scheme and in the sample are not great (Table 3). Overall, 80.5 per cent of the sample were single or widowed persons. Comparative figures from the warden survey were 73.5 per cent and 56.3 per cent respectively indicating that the ten selected schemes contained fewer married (couples) tenants than the average for Hanover schemes.

The average ages of the tenants interviewed ranged from 70 to 77 (Table 3) and the proportion of tenants over 80 from none to 33 per cent. The two schemes with the highest proportion of tenants over 80 also had the highest proportion of non-ambulant tenants (Caversham Park and Tewkesbury). However, the proportion of the most elderly and the non-ambulant in the sample was not as clearly related to the age of the scheme as perhaps one might have expected. There is a slight trend visible with none of the four schemes opened since 1973 having anyone over 80 in the sample, and only one (Cirencester I) having any non-ambulant tenants (two tenants, 13.3 per cent of sample).

The average length of residence of the tenants was clearly related to the age of the schemes, ranging from 0.7 years in the case of Royton II (opened 1975) to 6.1 for Cheltenham (opened 1968) (Table 3). The fact that the average age of the tenants was only weakly related to the age of the scheme suggests that Hanover have been reasonably successful in selecting a balanced group of tenants in terms of age.

PROFILES OF TEN HANOVER SCHEMES

In the ten profiles presented here, an attempt is made to provide the reader with some basic descriptive information that allows some useful comparisons of schemes, and components and characteristics of schemes to be made. Age, size, height, lifts, facilities, location, parking, views are some of the principal aspects that allow for comparison.

60

Profiles of ten Hanover schemes

Hanover House, off Maldwyn Avenue, Daubhill, Bolton, Lancashire

Hanover Gardens, Bracknell, Berkshire

Hanover Court, Caversham Park Village, Reading, Berkshire

Hanover Court, St. Stephen's Road, Cheltenham, Gloucestershire

Cambray Court, Chester Street, Cirencester, Gloucestershire

Hanover House, Pyenest Road, Halifax, Yorkshire

Hanover Court, Lee Street, Oldham, Lancashire

Royton Hall, Oldham Road, Royton, Lancashire

Ashetton-Bennett House, St. Marks Hill, Surbiton, Surrey

Hanover Court, Riverside Walk, Tewkesbury, Gloucestershire.

Acknowledgements

We wish to thank the Hanover Housing Association for providing photographs of the ten schemes, and the architects who provided plans upon which the sketches are based.

61

(i) Hanover House, off Maldwyn Avenue, Daubhill, Bolton, Lancashire
Year Built: 1971
Number Units: 29 single bedrooms
Number Tenants: 37

The site lies within an area of terraced housing and bungalows with, immediately adjacent, recently built council flats. On three sides there is housing with a public playing field on the fourth, whose boundary finishes close to the wall of one of the three two-storey blocks which comprise the scheme.

The layout of the site is such that the three blocks are not segregated from surrounding development by any physical structures such as fences or hedges. In fact, a public footpath runs through the centre of the scheme, dividing two of the blocks from the third. This footpath serves as a link between the surrounding housing and the nearby Leigh-Bolton main road, with its facilities for daily shopping and bus stops for access to Bolton town centre, two miles away.

No communal facilities are provided except for two outdoor seats between two of the blocks, and rotary driers are situated on the grassy areas within the 'functional' boundary of the scheme. There is parking space for two or three cars, but no garages are supplied.

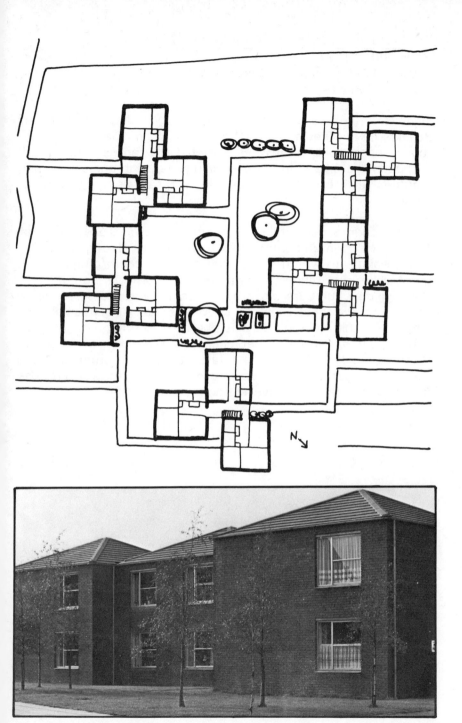

(ii) Hanover Gardens, Bracknell, Berkshire
Year Built: 1974
Number Units: 39 single bedrooms; 2 two bedrooms
Number Tenants: 52

Hanover Gardens is located on the wooded outskirts of Bracknell New Town, about three miles from the town centre itself, near to the busy Bracknell-Crowthorne main road. Although the site is in an area of new housing and continuing building, an effort has been made to retain as many trees as possible.

The scheme consists of a number of two storey rows of flats, with open balcony access to the upper floors, enclosing a quadrangle in which stands the common room/dining room, guest room and laundry room. Public footpaths do not cross the scheme, but pass close beside it, linking the surrounding housing to the local shopping centre, a walk of about half-an-hour. At this centre there is the nearest chemist and post office, but immediately adjacent to the site is a general store, a public house in the last stages of building, and a doctors' surgery. A garage is provided for the warden's use and parking space for several cars.

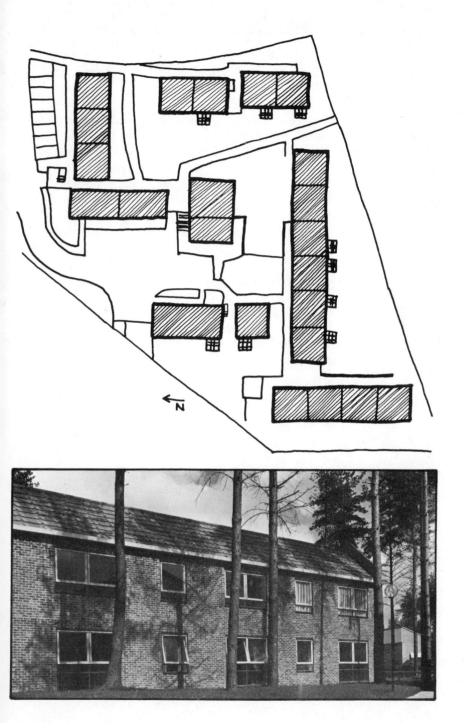

(iii)   Hanover   Court,   Caversham   Park   Village,   Reading,
Berkshire
Year Built: 1972
Number Units: 21 double bedrooms
Number Tenants: 25

The scheme is situated near a new shopping centre two miles
from Caversham Village and four miles from Reading town
centre.   The units are built as two storey open terraces with
stairways to the upper floors.   Detached private housing
stands nearby and a pathway to the adjacent shopping area
passes close to the flats. Although there is no common room,
laundry room or drying room, there is a guest room and
outdoor drying areas as well as parking space for about
twenty cars.

The main road to Reading is two hundred yards away and
shopping facilities are available immediately adjoining the
site; at one point thirty feet separates the shops from the
flats on the scheme.   A regular bus service provides access
both to Caversham and Reading town centre.

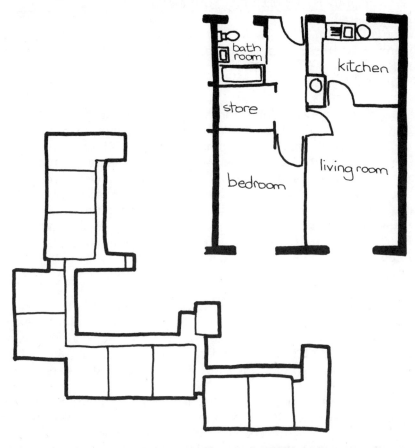

bath room

store

kitchen

bedroom

living room

(iv)   Hanover   Court,   St.   Stephen's   Road,   Cheltenham,
Gloucestershire
Year Built: 1968
Number Units: 30 single bedrooms; 8 double bedrooms; 3
bedsitters
Number Tenants: 41

The scheme consists of a large Regency house that has been converted into flatlets and bedsitters and which also contains the communal facilities (common room and drying room). The site is located one and a half miles from the town centre of Cheltenham and is situated to give views across the Cotswolds Hills in the distance to the south east. Around the site the well-wooded gardens of housing nearby provides a visual barrier to the traffic on the nearby A40 road. St. Stephen's Road itself, on which the scheme is situated, is quiet and pleasant normally, although used as a 'rat-run' by traffic at rush hours.

In the gardens of the house stand two newly built blocks of four-storey single bedroomed flats, with four units on each floor around a central service core. An access road runs along the side of the site, and car parking is available in two parking areas, catering for a total of about fifteen cars.

The nearest general store is a quarter of a mile away, a shopping centre at three quarters of a mile and town centre at $1\frac{1}{2}$ miles. The nearest church is one hundred yards while the post office is three quarters of a mile away. A bus stop is situated ten yards from the scheme.

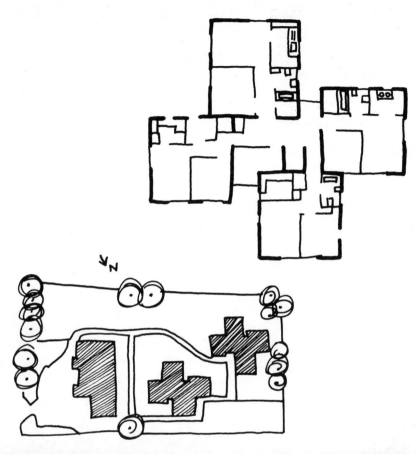

69

(v)   Cambray   Court,   Chester   Street,   Cirencester, Gloucestershire
Year Built: 1973
Number Units: 27 double bedrooms; 3 two bedrooms
Number Tenants: 40

The scheme is located within the built-up area, about six hundred yards from the town centre. It consists of two blocks, one of four floors with lift access, and three of two floors. The layout is arranged so that some tenants have quite spacious and well-managed garden plots.

A guest room, laundry room and small hobbies room are provided, but no common room or separate drying room, although a tumble drier is available in the laundry room. A tarmac parking area is provided for tenants' cars and a garage for the warden's use.

The main road passing alongside the scheme is not heavily used owing to the diversion of much traffic by a recently completed by-pass. A general store is approximately four hundred yards away and other facilities, including chemist, post office, church and doctor's surgery, are equally convenient.

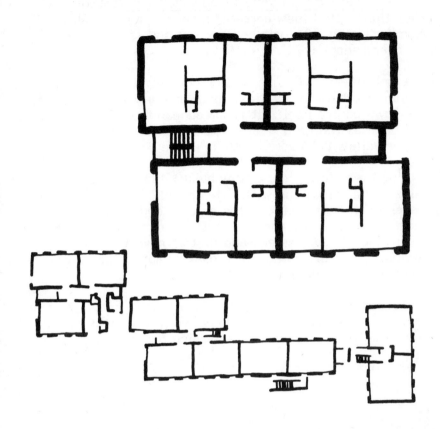

71

(vi) <u>Hanover House, Pyenest Road, Halifax, Yorkshire</u>
Year Built: 1971 (new eastern block completed January 1976)
Number Units: 58 single bedrooms; 1 double bedroom
Number Tenants: 72

The scheme lies on steeply sloping ground on the main road
running west out of Halifax, about one and a half miles from
the town centre itself. It is surrounded by housing of various
ages and as the ground slopes to the south, commands views
of the valley and moors which lie in the distance.

There are three, four-storey blocks, linked to each other by
covered balconies and with lifts as well as stairs serving the
upper floors. The back at the eastern end of the three is the
most recently built and contains a common room and guest
room and at the eastern end of this new block are outdoor
drying areas. Six garages and parking space for several cars
are also provided.

Access to shopping and other facilities is good, with nearby
general stores serving most daily needs, the local centre half
a mile away and a reliable bus service to Halifax.

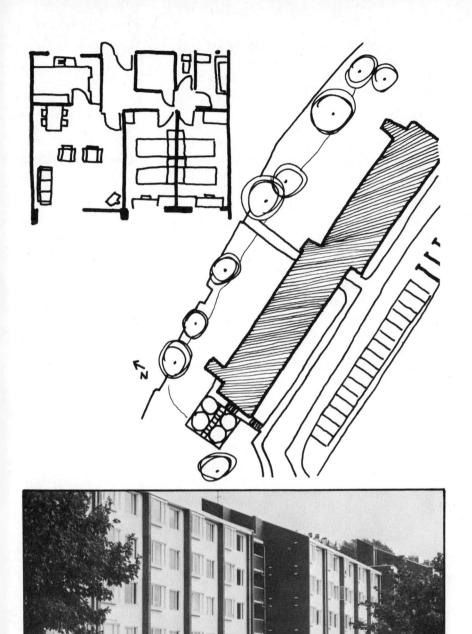

73

(vii) Hanover Court, Lee Street, Oldham, Lancashire
Year Built: 1973
Number Units: 26 double bedrooms
Number Tenants: 31

Hanover Court is located on the edge of Oldham's old core, half a mile from the town centre. It consists of a five-storey block, built on quite steeply sloping ground giving west-facing tenants a view of the woodlands and factories of Lancashire. To the east of the site an area of nineteenth century terraced housing and some small shops is awaiting demolition. There is also a junior school nearby with its playing fields and an area of small factories.

The main road to the town centre runs by the scheme and can be crossed by a pedestrian subway. Bus stops have been relocated to serve the scheme, but most needed facilities are easily accessible with the post office fifty yards away and a chemist and church equally convenient.

The only shared facility provided is a drying room, and there is car parking space for six cars, with a garage for the use of the warden.

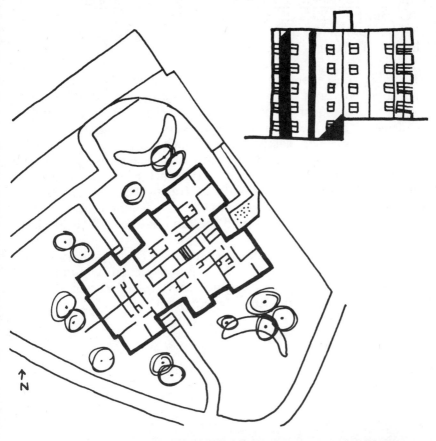

(viii) Royton Hall, Oldham Road, Royton, Lancashire
Year Built: 1975
Number Units: 28 double bedrooms; 2 two bedrooms
Number Tenants: 39

This site, the second to be built by Hanover in Royton, is just one hundred yards from the town centre, along the Rochdale Road.   It consists of four, two-storey blocks forming a landscaped court with a grassy mound planted with trees and flower beds. The design of the buildings is very similar to family flats nearby to the south and there is no physical boundary separating the two. A footpath running through the scheme is used by the tenants of these other buildings. To the west of the site is the main Oldham-Rochdale road, while between the site and this road the land has been left derelict.

A guest room has been provided. There are no other communal facilities apart from a laundry room which has not yet been equipped with plant at the time of survey. Accessibility to all facilities is excellent.

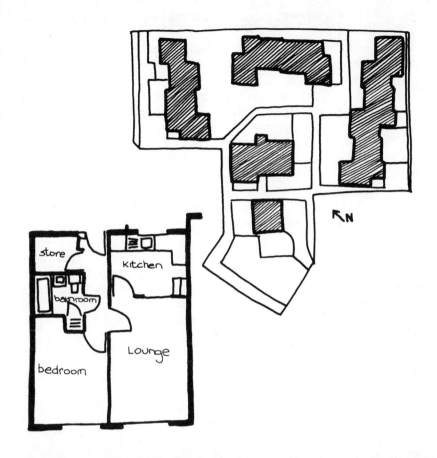

(ix) Ashetton-Bennett House, St. Marks Hill, Surbiton, Surrey
Year Built: 1968
Number Units: 18 single bedrooms; 8 double bedrooms
Number Tenants: 28

Surbiton is a suburban centre about ten miles south west of the centre of London. Hanover's housing scheme is built overlooking Surbiton town centre, on St. Marks Hill, one of the busy roads leading into the town centre. It is a five storey block (with lift access) surrounded by residential development on three sides and St. Marks Church and its grounds adjoining the scheme on the fourth side. It has its own well defined entrance and there is no through way for the public. Parking space is available for several cars.

Within the building a communal room is provided and rooms for drying clothes on all floors above ground level. The scheme is a quarter of a mile from Surbiton's centre reached either by a walk down the rather steep hill or by bus. The closeness of the centre means that all required facilities are very accessible.

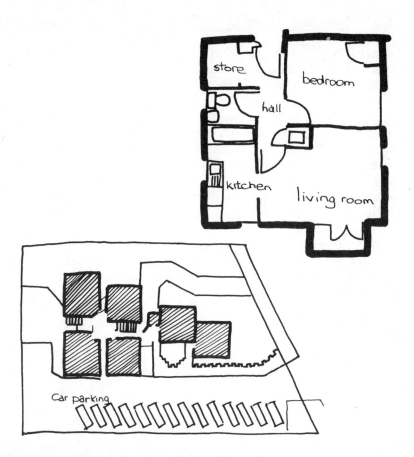

(x)   Hanover   Court,   Riverside   Walk,   Tewkesbury,
Gloucestershire
Year Built: 1972
Number Units: 29 double bedrooms
Number Tenants: 36

Hanover Court is built twenty yards from the main shopping
street in Tewkesbury, with a view of the flood plain of the
River Severn and, in the distance, the Malvern Hills. At the
north and east ends of the scheme lie the car park and service
road to the adjacent shops.   On the south side there are
pleasant secluded gardens, at the west end the scheme
overlooks the River Avon and a little-used service road.

   The building is a three-storey block (with lifts) which
contains an electric drying cabinet, but no other communal
facilities. Being so close to the town centre, accessibility to
all facilities is very good.

River Avon

Car Park

TENANT ATTITUDES

Tenants were given four different opportunities to express their general attitudes to the scheme. Firstly, they were asked to state how satisfied they were with their flats, using a scale number 1 to 5 (very unsatisfied to very satisfied). Then they were asked what they liked about their flats or these schemes in general and also what they disliked about them. Finally, at the end of the questionnaire, respondents were asked if they had any additional comments to make. The tenants' likes and dislikes are listed for each scheme in Tables 4 and 5.

Satisfaction

Overall, 85.1 per cent of the respondents said that they were satisfied or very satisfied with their flats, the average score ranging from 3.8 at Caversham Park (i.e. tenants just less than 'satisfied' on average) to 4.7 at Cheltenham (i.e. almost all tenants 'very satisfied'). Only five (3 per cent) tenants (three of them living in the Bracknell scheme) said they were dissatisfied to any great extent with their flats. The likes expressed by the tenants tended to be of a general nature and were shared by tenants in many schemes. The dislikes expressed by tenants were more specific in nature.

The most frequently mentioned feature was a good view or outlook comprising 14.2 per cent of the total replies. Halifax and Tewkesbury had the greatest number of mentions of this particular feature. The next most frequently mentioned features were location of the scheme in the town and the compactness of the flats. None of the eleven tenants referring to the location of the scheme lived on the Tewkesbury scheme. The comments on the compactness of the flats, along with the size of the rooms, the good design of the flats and the ease of running the flats were more widespread in all the schemes, and taken together formed the bulk of the 'likes'. 27 per cent of the 'likes' referred in some way to the design, layout or size of the flat.

Dissatisfaction

Adverse comments about the heating (and particularly the

cost) predominated. They were common to all the schemes, although at Cirencester (ceiling heating) and at Bracknell (storage heating) more tenants complained about the expense of the heating. At Royton three tenants complained about the expense of the heating. At Royton three tenants specifically mentioned the fact that the heating was switched off in summer. The second most frequent complaint related to a poor view. However, the Halifax scheme accounted for half the complaints, apparently reflecting tenants' reactions to the untidiness of part of the site. Complaints about high rents or rates (mainly the latter) were not confined to any one scheme. Similarly, the comments about window design and operation problems were general. Complaints about the bathrooms being located in the middle of the flat, and, therefore, having no windows and requiring artificial ventilation were obviously confined to the two schemes at Royton and Cirencester with these built-in features. Another complaint was about the alleged poor construction or finish. The Tewkesbury scheme was most frequently mentioned in this regard.

General comments

Overall, the most frequently mentioned general comments reflected the tenants' satisfaction with their home and scheme. Several of the comments related to specific problems, some of which have already been mentioned, such as poor appearance of the site on the Halifax scheme. A number of tenants at the Bracknell scheme commented on the need for a local chemist and post office, and expressed the desire for some private gardens. Two more general comments deserve a mention. Firstly, the cleaning and operation of windows remains a source of complaint. Secondly, there were (predictably in our view) unsolicited comments made about wardens by nine tenants in all. The comments came from tenants in four schemes and were of no significance in the context of this study.

ANALYSIS OF TENANT RESPONSE

The analysis of tenant response considers each of the six main issues addressed by the questionnaires, i.e. heating, noise, safety, communal facilities, privacy and location. Specific design recommendations are made which derive directly from this study of the ten schemes. General recommendations are also made which derive from the literature. A number of issues are identified which clearly need to be researched further, in some cases by means of experimental features in new schemes.

Heating

Heating was identified by the wardens as the second most unsatisfactory aspect of schemes. Of the different heating systems, gas warm air and electric ceiling heating received the most unfavourable comments from the wardens (Interim Report, p. 9). This concern about the type and cost of heating is reflected in the unsolicited criticisms made before heating had been mentioned to the tenants. Tenants were asked to indicate their satisfaction with the heating of their flats on a scale from 1 (very unsatisified) to 5 (very satisfied). Table 9 lists the average satisfaction with heating for each of the schemes. Four schemes had average scores of 3 or less (i.e. the neutral point and below).

Two of these schemes (Bracknell and Caversham Park) had electric storage heaters, one (Oldham) had underfloor electric storage and the scheme with the lowest average rating (Cirencester) had electric ceiling heating. Table 9 also illustrates the differences in rating between the systems and the scores for the heating systems have been grouped together. Two points emerge: firstly, the low average satisfaction with electric ceiling heating and secondly the high score for gas central heating (Royton scheme only). The reasons may be explained by answers given by tenants to additional questions.

The first question asked tenants whether the main heating system was sufficient to keep them warm during the day and during the night (Table 9). The two gas-fired systems (warm air, and central heating) appeared to be effective, whereas 38 per cent of tenants with electric underfloor storage heating said they were not warm enough during the day or night. One problem with the storage systems in cold weather (as illustrated by the electric underfloor heating) appears to be

84

that during the day when they are 'running down' they are no longer sufficiently effective.

Tenants were also asked if they used any additional supplementary source of heating (Table 6). 53 per cent of the tenants having gas central heating said they did, the majority using the supplementary heating in summer only when the central heating was turned off. The proportion rose to between 70 per cent and 80 per cent of the tenants having gas warm air, electric underfloor and electric storage heating. The main reasons evidently being the need to supplement the main heating system in very cold weather, or in the afternoons and early evening before the storage heating came on. 96 per cent of the tenants having electric ceiling heating said that they used additional heating, almost half giving the reason that the ceiling heating was too expensive or was not liked, i.e. implying that they did not use the main heating system.

This latter conclusion is underlined in the responses to the question on whether tenants usually used the main heating system (Table 7). The number is negligible for all systems except electric ceiling heating which 72 per cent of tenants said they did not usually use. This percentage is high partly because the new section of the Halifax scheme which had ceiling heating has only been occupied for about three months, and some tenants said that it had not been cold enough yet to use the ceiling heating. In addition, some tenants have not used their ceiling heating, saying that it is too expensive although they have not yet used it or had any heating bills, i.e. there is a strong belief among tenants that ceiling heating is expensive which has led to its non-use.

Nevertheless, 67 per cent of the tenants on the Cirencester scheme (where there is ceiling heating and in which most tenants have lived for about three years) stated that they did not use this system. This degree of non-use is serious, both because it represents a waste of money and resources and because of the attendant risk to life which must arise when tenants attempt to save by not using the heating system provided. There is the danger from appliances provided by tenants and conversely the risk of hypothermia.

The costs of heating may be fully compared for eight of the schemes in which tenants were paying an all-inclusive electricity payment for heating, lighting and cooking. A small number of tenants who paid for cooking by a coin box have been included as the difference in amount was only marginal (e.g. an error of about 5 per cent). The two schemes in which heating was paid for separately were Surbiton and Royton, the two gas-fired systems. Both these systems appear relatively cheap, but account should be taken of the likely use of additional (electric) heating used in these schemes, particularly in the Surbiton scheme.

The electric systems averaged out at £43.30 per quarter (£3.33 per week) for underfloor heating; £46.20 (£3.55) for electric storage and £55.64 (£4.28) for electric ceiling heating. The averages hide a wide variation between the tenants who were paying between £1.50 and £7.50 per week for their electricity with 46 of the tenants (37 per cent of those giving information) paying over £50 per quarter (£3.85 per week).

It was expected that there would be a large number of comments about the cost of heating because shortly before the survey the cost of heating for the elderly had become a national issue.

Tenants were, therefore, asked if they felt that their particular heating system was more expensive than others, given that all prices of heating had risen recently. Predictably, 71 per cent of those with electric ceiling heating at Cirencester answered in the affirmative. In Table 8 the amount tenants paid for their heating is related to whether they felt it was more expensive than average. Those tenants who felt their heating was more expensive than average were indeed in general paying more for their heating; 13 tenants were paying over £60 per quarter compared with only four tenants paying over £60 who felt their heating was not more expensive. The average payment for those who felt it was more expensive was of the order of £52 per quarter, whereas for the remaining tenants it was £44 per quarter (excluding those paying for gas only). Tenants were invited to make any additional comments. They included:

86

Gas warm air - Heat does not reach all rooms.
Electric underfloor - Satisfied; need insulation on windows (double glazing); heat insufficient in the afternoons/evenings before heating comes on; immersion heating expensive.
Electric ceiling - Inefficient; expensive; good all round heat.
Gas central heating - Immersion heating expensive, why not connect to central heating?
Electric storage - Satisfied; storage heaters bulky; expensive.

It should be noted that not all the comments were negative. Satisfaction and praise for the heating systems was frequently expressed.

Since the previous Hanover study which dealt extensively with heating systems, one new type of heating system has been installed in Hanover developments - electric ceiling heating - and it seems appropriate to concentrate upon this system because the satisfaction and the faults of the other types of heating largely reflect those found in the earlier study. We would also agree that efficiency, low running cost and easy control of heating are the most important criteria for evaluating the heating system.

Clearly, the rising cost of energy has had and will continue to have important consequences. There is no doubt that ceiling heating may be effective when properly used. However, high running costs have compelled many tenants to stop using it all the time, and in many cases to rely on their own bar fires or convector heaters. The running costs of heating systems have become the critical factor influencing behaviour and degree of use. The fact that ceiling heating may be effective and subject to control is clearly of much less importance than its high cost. Many tenants are voting with their feet and the consequences could be serious.

Gas central heating emerged as the most preferred system in terms of both cost (tenants had few complaints partly because heating charges were included with the rent), and heating the flats effectively

Electric storage heaters were rated slightly higher than electric underfloor heating, although comments about their bulk and cost and difficulties of control were common on the two schemes where storage heaters were not rated highly (Bracknell and Caversham Park).

It was not possible to compare different systems of paying for heating as the majority of tenants paid by quarterly electricity bills. On only two schemes were payments made in the rent, and in both cases this appeared to work well. In view of the high and rising cost of heating, tenants should be assisted by the introduction of a system of more frequent payments.

Noise

Noise was selected as an issue for further study because over a quarter of the wardens felt that noise insulation in the schemes was unsatisfactory. However, the proportion of tenants who said that they were bothered by noise was somewhat lower - 24 per cent (Table 11). Only in one scheme, Tewkesbury, located in a town centre, did the proportion of tenants bothered by noise rise to about 40 per cent.

A similar proportion of tenants (25 per cent) said that they could hear their neighbour's TV or radio. The tenants who said they could hear the TV were not always the same ones who were bothered by noise, in fact, 61 per cent of those who said they could hear the TV were not bothered by noise at all.

Just over half the sources of noise which caused the complaints were external sources; road traffic, commercial or industrial activity, or people (Table 11). Of the internal sources of noise by far the most frequently mentioned were upstairs neighbours (i.e. noise through the ceiling) followed by noises associated with the lift and banging doors. The types of noise obviously reflect the noise sources - the non-specific noises (e.g. intermittent rumbling, etc.) emanating from sources such as lifts and nearby commercial buildings. One feature about the noises is that a large proportion of them are continuous or frequent noises occurring throughout the day. This particularly applies to traffic noise. The night

88

time is a sensitive period accounting for a quarter of the specified noises. The evidence suggests that internal noise insulation is not a critical problem in the ten schemes examined. Almost two-thirds of the tenants who said they could hear their neighbour's TV (25 per cent of all tenants) were not bothered by this. In other words, a certain amount of noise was expected if it was recognised as being necessary (there were a number of references to the neighbours being somewhat deaf). It was the 'unnecessary' internal noises which caused concern - creaking floor boards, banging doors, and lift noises.

The location of the scheme is obviously critical for external noise, although nowhere did the problem appear acute enough to suggest solutions such as double glazing. Indeed, tenants at Tewkesbury, for example, were probably aware of the trade-off between good accessibility to shops and services, and the associated noise problem.

Safety

Two aspects of safety appeared critical from the analysis of the warden survey - fire safety and the alarm call system. It was felt that it would not be useful to pursue the fire safety issue with the tenants (with the risk of alarming them) and the questionnaire, therefore, concentrated on the alarm system and the design of the flat from the safety point of view.

One important aspect of design for safety is whether the need for such design is recognised or resented, for this may have an influence on the design effectiveness. For example, alarm call cords may be tied up out of the way if they are not felt to be necessary; extra shelves put in at an excessive height, etc. Two questions were, therefore, asked about the necessity of an alarm and safety design feature:

Question	Yes	No
Is an alarm system necessary?	156 (97.5%)	4
Are there too many safety features?	4	156

89

97.5 per cent of tenants thought the alarm system was necessary, and only 2.5 per cent felt that there were too many safety features. It is sometimes assumed that the elderly resent such 'unpleasant reminders of their declining independence', but the evidence in the table does not support this view.

In order to check on the effectiveness of the alarm call systems installed in the schemes, tenants were asked whether they had ever used the alarm, how often in the last 12 months, and whether it had been effective in summoning help.

22 per cent of tenants interviewed had used the alarm at some time, 83 per cent of them in the last twelve months. 70 per cent of them had used the alarm only once or twice, and no one had used the alarm more than five times in the year. This rate of use of the alarm is considerably less than in the survey of wardens' duties carried out by Boldy on a sample of Devon schemes, in which he found wardens spending an average of half an hour per week answering emergency calls (or almost one call per scheme per week). (Boldy, 1973)

This difference in use may reflect the emphasis put by Hanover on the 'active elderly', but the existing population is ageing and inevitably over time the number and incidence of calls must increase. Only three persons who had used the alarm said it had not been effective. In two cases, this was the result of a technical fault. In the third case, the tenant was deaf and had difficulty using the intercom system. This latter problem was also mentioned in response to the question to all tenants as to whether this alarm system was easy to use and what problems, if any, they had with it (Table 12).

There was no significant difference between the two main systems in the proportion of tenants who said that it was not easy to use. The main problem is the worry that tenants have about not being able to reach the alarm in the case of an accident, particularly if not all rooms are connected to the alarm or if a room is large and has just one activation point. This problem is common to most types of alarm except the portable types which can be constantly carried - and these have other major disadvantages.

90

Although the use of alarm systems could increase with the age of the schemes (and hence the average age of the tenants) the evidence suggests that the present systems are adequate.

Another problem mentioned was the ease with which the alarm can be mistaken for a light switch (particularly by visitors). The use of different materials or colours would be helpful. Although this may make the alarm system 'overt', the evidence suggests that the tenants increasingly require reassurance as they grow older. The intercom system received few comments: unreliability which is a reflection of its greater complexity, and partly to the need for frequent checks; inability to use the intercom because it had never been explained; and finally, the difficulty which the deaf and hard of hearing had in using the system effectively, i.e. it is reduced to being a one-way communication and this fact must be recognised in the design of operating procedures.

In order to obtain residents' reactions to the design of their flats from the point of view of safety, they were first asked to rate their dwellings on a three point scale where 1 was badly designed and 3 was well designed. The average scores are all above the mid-point, i.e. the flats were thought to be fairly well designed. Three schemes had over 15 per cent of tenants who felt that their schemes were badly designed for safety; Bracknell, where bathroom problems seemed to predominate; Oldham where among the problems mentioned poor lighting was the most frequent; and Surbiton, where high cupboards were the reason for the negative responses.

The tenants' comments and suggestions for design improvements are summarised for all the schemes in Table 10. Most frequently mentioned was the difficulty of cleaning windows easily, and cupboards which were too high to reach easily (see Literature Review for recommended heights). Bathrooms were the next most frequently mentioned. The grab pole alongside the bath in some cases becomes slippery when wet. Four tenants mentioned that the bath was too small (this is really an example of a safety feature which some tenants feel is unnecessary) and the same number said that a shower would be preferable to a bath. Apart from the high cupboards, which refers specifically to the Surbiton

91

scheme, the other questions raised, reflect individual preferences and sometimes difficulties which tenants have, rather than specific design faults. This represents considerable success in designing with safety criteria in mind.

Communal facilities

Five types of communal facilities were provided on some of the ten sampled schemes: laundry, drying room, guest room, common room and hobbies room. In the wardens' survey one of the most frequent comments was the lack of any communal facilities, and yet there is evidence both from the wardens' survey and from the previous Hanover study, that facilities provided are often under used. It was, therefore, decided not just to investigate the level of use and demand for the different facilities, but also to explore the behavioural influences which affect the use of such facilities. By understanding these influences it is hoped that a sounder basis for deciding on the provision of communal facilities can be found.

Laundry and drying rooms   It was hypothesised that the use and demand of both these facilities would depend upon the tenants' ownership of a working washing machine and/or a drier; the facilities (e.g. launderette) in the neighbourhood; the tenants' normal mode of doing their washing and also the equipment provided in the laundry and drying rooms. Although the data partly demonstrates this, it is not possible to say which influences are most important, or to say how much tenants have adapted to a situation against their preferences.

Almost one in three tenants own washing machines in the ten schemes. One might expect the ownership of machines to be lower in the schemes which had laundry facilities (Bracknell and Cirencester), but this is not the case. The examination of how tenants do their washing and the use made of the laundries shows that even when laundry facilities are provided, at least as many tenants do all or part of their own washing in their flats as use the laundry facilities.

48 per cent of the tenants of Bracknell and 40 per cent of those in Cirencester used the laundry room once a week or

more. The reasons given for not using the laundry by tenants (Table 15) includes the comment that they are 'too crowded' which implies that the laundry rooms are operating at or near capacity with the present usage. Considering all the schemes together, 45 per cent of tenants did their own washing (both in sinks, etc. and in washing machines), and 13 per cent used local launderettes. The proportion who used launderettes rose to 53 per cent in the Royton scheme, and 42 per cent of the tenants in Surbiton did part of their washing in a launderette. Thus, the presence of launderette facilities in the area does have a marked effect on the way in which tenants do their own washing.

The two schemes which have a laundry have a higher per centage of tenants saying that a laundry is necessary on the scheme (Table 13). The proportion varies on the other schemes, from 23.1 per cent on the Surbiton scheme to over 80 per cent on the Oldham and Royton schemes. The number saying it is required is not related to the ownership of washing machines at all, nor is it connected with the existence of a drying room on the scheme.

The laundry rooms on the two schemes were apparently well used, although there was a substantial proportion of tenants who either did not do their own washing, or preferred to do it in their own flats. An increase in the size of the laundry facilities might attract additional users. The distance to the laundry room was a deterrent for some.

In contrast to the substantial use of laundries, the drying rooms were not well used (Table 14) with over 90 per cent of the tenants on the Oldham and Surbiton schemes using the drying rooms less than once a fortnight.

Only the drying room of the Cheltenham scheme was used once a week or more by more than a quarter of the tenants. Part of the reason for this is the higher ownership of some form of drier; 54.3 per cent of the total number of tenants had a drier, almost twice as many as had washing machines. It is, therefore, not surprising that having their own drier was one of the most frequently given reasons for not using the drying room (Table 14). The second reason stems from the inconvenience of separating the washing and drying processes - reasons such as too far away, upstairs, etc. The other response, apart from using their own driers, was that all the washing and drying was done at the launderette.

Despite the low usage of the drying rooms on two of the schemes having them, over 60 per cent of the respondents felt the room was necessary, and including all the other schemes, an average of 61 per cent felt a drying room was necessary.

In summary, whilst the drying rooms hardly appear to be justified by present levels of use, the laundry rooms in the two cases studied were. There is a strong case for a laundry which includes drying machines as well as washing machines in those schemes which are not located close to launderettes. However good the communal facilities provided there will still be a proportion of tenants who are not able, or do not wish, to use the facilities. There is some evidence to suggest that if quality equipment is provided for washing and drying, at low running costs, at a conveniently located spot, especially in multi-storey accommodation, the level of usage is considerable. The other factor to be reflected in design is that central facilities release space in the flat for other uses.

Guest room Six of the ten sampled schemes had a guest room provided, and an average of 20 per cent of tenants had used the room in the last year (Table 16a). The highest rate of usage was on the Cirencester scheme in which 47 per cent of the tenants had used the guest room, and the lowest rate was the Royton scheme which only opened in 1975. The Halifax rate is also low, but with 93 per cent of the tenants originating locally the number of visitors staying the night is likely to be low (Table 19). It is of interest, however, that on these six schemes, 22 per cent of the tenants had had someone to stay in their own flats. Only in the two schemes which had relatively high usage of guest rooms (Caversham Park and Cirencester) did the number of tenants using the guest room exceed the number using their own flat for visitors.

In the four schemes which did not have a guest room a similar proportion (22 per cent) had had someone to stay in

94

their flats - the majority utilising some kind of temporary bed or divan in their living rooms. A further 14.5 per cent had wanted to have someone to stay, but had been prevented by the lack of a guest room. When asked whether they felt a guest room was necessary, just over half the tenants in the four schemes said it was, compared with 84 per cent in the six schemes which already had a guest room.

The high percentage of those in the six schemes saying a guest room is needed has to be contrasted in some schemes with the number who put up visitors in their own rooms despite the guest room. If account is taken too of the fact that most stays were of relatively short duration (3 days or less) then even if all tenants were to use the guest room it would remain empty for most of the year. On the other hand, there are occasions when a guest room would be invaluable (accommodation of temporary nursing help for example) and a guest room could be more readily justified if its use could be combined with some additional function. Account must be taken in new developments of the likely demand for visitors. One of the main factors is the location of the tenants with respect to their friends and family - those schemes which contain a high proportion of local tenants have fewer overnight stays - day trips predominate, e.g. Halifax, Bolton, Oldham, all have over 80 per cent of tenants originating locally and also have few visitors - under 15 per cent having had someone to stay. Four schemes have under one third of tenants originating locally, and have a higher proportion of visitors - Bracknell, Cirencester, Royton and Tewkesbury.

Common room   The issue of common room provision is complex not only because of the different expectations of what a common room is for, but also because the common room depends as much upon the attitudes and aptitude of the wardens and tenants as it does upon design features. The questionnaire, was, therefore, designed to find out how common rooms were used when provided, and what tenants felt they should be used for where they had wanted one and they were not provided. In addition, information about tenants' social contacts both inside and out of the schemes was collected to see if they were related in any way to common room provision.

Four schemes had a common room (Table 18a) and the rate of usage varied widely among the four schemes. On the Surbiton and Bracknell schemes over half the tenants used the common room more than once a week. The Cheltenham scheme common room was scarcely used at all. Examining the activities which the tenants engaged in when they use the common room, it can be seen that on average well over three quarters of the activities are organised ones - coffee mornings, bingo, films, whist drives, club afternoons, tenants' meetings, etc. Informal activities such as reading, conversation, sewing or playing cards formed the remaining activities. With high individual ownership of TV sets the common rooms do not function as TV rooms as in many other schemes reviewed in the literature survey.

The high proportion of organised activities taking place and expected of the common rooms highlights the dependence on the warden's ability and willingness to organise. The scheme which had few organised events (Cheltenham) had the lowest use of common room, and also the lowest proportion of tenants (among the four schemes with a common room) who said a common room was necessary. On the other three schemes, all tenants said the common room was necessary. In the schemes without a common room, this percentage ranged from 27 per cent in Cirencester to 85 per cent in Oldham.

An interesting difference between use and expected use emerges from the question as to what tenants wanted a common room for. 53 per cent (21 tenants) of the tenants replying in the schemes without a common room said that they wanted the room for general socialising, i.e. non-organised activities. 42 per cent (17 tenants) said that they would want the common room for organised activities. This is a completely different balance between organised and non-organised activities compared with the actual use of common rooms, which perhaps suggests that tenants are not very realistic about their aspirations.

To investigate whether the common rooms had an influence on internal social contacts and visiting, tenants were asked for an estimate of the number of tenants they knew by name, and also the number they had visited, or had been visited by,

96

in the last week. There is no significant difference in the percentage of tenants known and visited between the groups of schemes with and without common rooms. There is wide variation between the schemes, but the reason must be looked for elsewhere. There is, for example, a tendency for the proportion of tenants known to fall with increasing size of scheme. However, there are some exceptions to the trend, indicating that other influences are important. When tenants were asked whether there was enough social contact on the schemes, 91 per cent of the tenants who had a common room said that there was, compared with 68 per cent of those on schemes without a common room.

These findings tend to confirm the view that the role of the common room is a place primarily for organised events rather than informal contact. The amount of social contact in the two types remains broadly comparable, though tenants living in schemes without common rooms are not able to share in organised entertainment or meetings with other tenants. Although it was thought that tenants with previous ties with the area and without a common room might have more outside links reflected in visits to friends and relatives and to churches, clubs, theatres, etc. the average number of weekly outside activities in which tenants took part appeared insensitive to either factor.

The summarised list of outside activities (Table 20) shows that attendance at church is still the most frequent activity, followed by pensioners' and social clubs. The conclusion we reach is that the provision of a common room extends choice and opportunity to tenants who may wish to organise social and other events together. It removes the necessity to make some trips for such purposes, but on the other hand, people may well be able to extend their circle of friends and visiting habits as a result of a lively programme of 'in-house' common room activities. No mechanical relationships can be established. There is no evidence to suggest that the provision of a common room leads to withdrawal of the elderly from external contacts. On the contrary, there is a demand for common rooms where none exist and they are much appreciated where they are provided. They appear to be desirable to tenants irrespective of accessibility to other facilities and other activities that might be considered 'competitive'. We draw the conclusion that they meet a characteristically unique need and provide for activities the quality and extent of which depend on the organising abilities available, not least the warden.

Hobbies room   Only one scheme had what was officially described as a hobbies room (Cirencester) although on the Bracknell scheme the communal hall was regarded by tenants as a hobbies room. In the former case the room was scarcely used (only 20 per cent of the tenants used it) because the room was so small. In fact, it was used as a store for gardening equipment because of its small size. On the Bracknell scheme about 60 per cent of the tenants used the communal hall over once a week. The reason for the especially high usage of this facility seems to be the high level of motivation among the tenants themselves. Although the warden is actively involved with the tenants and encourages social activities, it is the tenants who organised regular bingo, whist and keep fit evenings and who, through the efforts of their own committee, have also gathered funds to pay for outings to the coast, excursions and trips to night-time social events.

It is clear that a hobbies room will not be used if it is not of suitable design or size for the activities for which it is intended. In view of the large number of single women in schemes and the hobbies which are popular with the tenants (e.g. knitting, needlework, etc.), it is unlikely that any other than an easily adaptable multi-function room would command sufficient use except in the case of a large scheme.

Dining room   It is appropriate here to mention the fact that Bracknell is at present the only Hanover scheme which has had equipment installed to enable cooking to be done on the premises, so that the common/hobbies room becomes a dining room too.

Although no specific questions were asked about this dining room, discussion with the tenants and the warden suggests that the dining facilities are not really well used. About 10-15 tenants usually use the room daily out of a total of 52 tenants. Nevertheless, the small number of tenants who regularly eat in the dining hall would be disappointed if the facilities were to be discontinued. The majority of the people on the scheme either prefer to cook for themselves at home or do not wish to arrange their day so that they are on the premises at the time of the meal. It is not known how many people would have to use the facilities in order to make it economically viable, but the hall provided has seating accommodation for only about thirty tenants, so this is the maximum that would ever be able to use the room for meals at one time.

Privacy

The warden survey drew attention to the loss of privacy that can result from the siting of schemes in residential areas where there may be pedestrian rights of way or grounds used by children as play spaces.

Tenants were asked whether the location of the scheme was too private, about right, or not private enough. Overall, 80 per cent of tenants felt their scheme was sufficiently private. Only 2 per cent felt a sense of isolation. At Bolton, 33 per cent and Royton 67 per cent of tenants felt there was insufficient privacy, which related to the fact that children played in the grounds and that people used the grounds as a short cut. On the other hand, at Bracknell and Oldham, only 5 per cent and 23 per cent of tenants respectively were actually bothered about children playing compared with the much larger number of 43 per cent and 54 per cent who noticed them playing.

Tenants were asked whether they wanted to make any changes to the scheme to make it more or less private. An average of 25 per cent of tenants wanted the schemes made more private, the proportion ranging from over 60 per cent on the Oldham and Royton schemes to less than 10 per cent on the Halifax, Surbiton and Tewkesbury schemes. At Royton the presence of children playing and the extent of intrusion of people within the schemes clearly constituted a nuisance and an invasion of privacy for many tenants.

The most frequent suggestion was that the boundaries of the scheme should be indicated in some way, whether by means of a solid barrier or fence or merely a nominal boundary or hedge. Various other suggestions were made to prevent people taking short cuts through private grounds. There may be remedial measures that could be taken to reduce invasion of privacy and nuisance. There are siting and design implications worth noting also in respect of future schemes.

Location

The warden survey confirmed the view that locational questions and especially distance from the chemist's shop and town centre are critical factors. The sample of ten schemes was chosen to include a range of locations with respect to the town centre. At Royton, Surbiton and Tewkesbury, schemes were located in or very close to the town centre and all tenants stated that their homes were 'very conveniently' located. The Bolton scheme, located two miles from the centre, with chemist, general store and post office within a quarter of a mile was similarly rated. Only Bracknell, which although very close to a general store, was a mile from a post office and chemist, and over two miles from the centre, was considered less conveniently located.

If the cluster of essential facilities is provided nearby, then the distance of the town centre appears acceptable. It should be noted that six of the schemes were more than a quarter of a mile from a general store or a post office and five of these were judged to be less than very convenient by the tenants. The tenants were asked where they normally did their shopping and how often (Table 21). The percentage of tenants using the town centre and shopping there twice a week or more, is clearly dependent upon the distance or accessibility of the town centre.

It is clear that the closeness of a general store or post office to the Halifax, Oldham and Bracknell schemes does not make up for the other absent facilities.

At Bolton 91 per cent of tenants visit the centre by bus at a much reduced rate for pensioners which is no doubt why the centre is considered convenient. By contrast, 86 per cent of tenants at Bracknell, about the same distance from the centre, visit the centre by bus without any comparable

100

reductions. Not surprisingly, tenants rated the convenience to the centre itself much lower. The reason that so many travel to the centre despite the distance and cost is partly due to the lack of facilities locally, and partly, where these do exist, the difficulty of reaching them by public transport. The nearby local centre is too far away for many of the tenants to walk, but is not served by the buses that pass by the scheme. In only four of the schemes did anyone wish to be nearer the town centre. 41 per cent of the tenants on the Bracknell scheme and 29 per cent on the Cheltenham scheme would have preferred a location more accessible to the centre, which merely confirms the importance of convenient and cheap bus services, especially for shopping trips.

The car ownership rate for each scheme ranges from 30 per cent of tenants at Tewkesbury, to none in Bolton, Caversham, Cheltenham and Royton. Of the 164 tenants interviewed only 13 (7.9 per cent) had cars.

Respondents were asked to rate the convenience of the schemes to a post office, and to a church. The perceived convenience to a post office is clearly related to distance (Table 24). Schemes with a post office closer than about half a mile are reckoned to be convenient on average, those between half and three quarters of a mile neither convenient nor inconvenient (score of 3) and those over (Bracknell - 1 mile) as inconvenient. The responses for convenience to a church are similar,although the existence of different denominations makes the distance measured to the nearest church less useful. However, the church is still the most frequently used facility, excepting shopping and close location is therefore important. So far only the distance to various facilities has been considered and the accessibility of the centres by bus. For trips in the immediate vicinity walking is the most important mode of movement and distance is just one of the factors which affect ease of walking to a facility. Respondents were asked if there were any problems of walking in their areas, and if so, what they were (Table 23).

On three schemes over half the respondents said there were local problems to easy mobility. At Cirencester, poor pavement conditions made walking difficult; at Oldham, there

101

were problems of crossing the road; and at Bracknell, the lack of pavements, steep slopes and traffic combined to make walking difficult. Taking all the schemes together, three problems were predominant:

(i)   traffic and difficulties in crossing the road - subways provided in some cases not being used because of steps, slopes or fear of attack

(ii)   steep inclines, which are difficult to avoid in towns, such as Halifax, where topography is varied

(iii)   the poor condition or lack of pavements; the fear or likelihood of falling on uneven pavements is real for the elderly and may prevent or deter them from going out.

Finally, tenants were asked what facilities they felt were not provided, if any. Table 25 lists the responses. Over half the respondents at Bracknell and Oldham - the latter being partly related to the impending demolition of the local shops - mentioned various shopping facilities. Interestingly, on the schemes which were well served by shopping facilities, entertainment facilities were mentioned, (e.g. Bolton, Caversham Park, Surbiton).

The responses overall show that the post office, chemist and fresh food shops were the most frequently mentioned facilities, followed by other types of shops and library facilities. This confirms yet again the importance to the elderly of the post office (for pensions), chemist (for medicaments) and fresh food shops (for everyday needs and an alternative to frozen or tinned food).

5 Conclusions and recommendations

INTRODUCTION

The conclusions and recommendations are again organised under the four headings which most appropriately relate to operational issues and methods of implementation.

(i)   Design improvements
(ii)   Location requirements
(iii)   Management, and
(iv)   General policy issues

The conclusions draw on evidence from both surveys and work discussed and listed in Part II of the study.

DESIGN IMPROVEMENTS

The warden's dwelling

Wardens in Hanover's schemes require an office, for both the growing volume of administrative and liaison functions they are called upon to do, and also because they need a place to meet visitors who include medical and social service personnel of many kinds as well as relatives of tenants. Functional separation of private living area from the area necessary to carry out the duties associated with the job together with a separate telephone system which can be switched over to the office or a deputy's flat when the warden is off duty are minimum requirements in our view. It is worth noting that Hanover have included offices for wardens in ten of their schemes already, and the evidence suggests that this has been both a worthwhile development and a development which should become the norm.

Hanover defines the role and duties of its wardens, but generally the role of the warden on sheltered housing schemes remains ambiguous and ill-defined. Recent research has been

103

attempted to examine and analyse the perceptions which different 'players' entertain of the warden's role in the sheltered housing field. Empirical study of what wardens actually do; the tendency for their role and work load to grow in both a qualitative as well as quantitative sense; requires a reappraisal of their minimum requirements so that a functionally separate office area, extra storage space and a garage become a standard provision in sheltered housing schemes. There are closely related issues which touch upon the supportive, administrative and managerial role of the warden which are not primarily design issues. These are of critical importance and stand between policy formation on the one hand and the physical design expression of such policies on the other. We return to these issues at various points in the chapter.

Community facilities

Laundry and drying rooms A substantial number of tenants will always prefer to do at least some of their washing in their own flats. Nevertheless, communal facilities remain essential. There is more justification for providing a laundry room than a drying room. On schemes where laundry rooms were provided they were well used. The installation of a drier in the same room as the washing machines would attract more tenants and avoid the necessity for some people who are relatively less mobile to use local launderettes. Location is critical.

For elderly people a walk of even a few yards carrying heavy items to be washed can be tiring and an effective deterrent to use. It is relevant that at the Halifax schemes where tenants had to use lifts and walk some distance to reach rotary driers, they were little used. A central position with covered access is a minimum requirement and the evidence of a few instances of vandalism suggests that facilities need to be relatively easily kept under surveillance.

Guest room The level of usage of guest rooms is generally low and it may not always be cost-effective to provide a self-contained purpose-built unit. The introduction of multi-use accommodation requires the formulation of a number of experimental design briefs and controlled building experiments. The provision of a multi-purpose flexible unit situated at ground level and capable of intermittent use by the partially disabled and those temporarily ill combined with a free standing shower unit might also provide accommodation for a relief warden or nursing help. Such a unit might also be used by the occasional visitor. The warden's growing supportive as well as managerial role may be reflected in the way such flexible and adaptive spaces are provided in the future.

Common room The hobbies room, dining room, and common room may usefully be combined within a flexible and adaptable multi-purpose building space. It may be that in any specific scheme, requirements will vary.

Guidelines in terms of space standards related to the size of schemes would be helpful, though size is not the only critical variable. The quality of space, finishes and inherent possibilities of adaptation to meet a variety of needs throughout the day and evening may well influence decisively the level of usage. In one scheme, a large room sufficient to seat all the tenants was used only once a week. In another scheme, better use would have been made of the room if it had been big enough both to seat more at some times and small enough to seat less at other times. The obvious conclusion is to provide flexibility. A large room could be subdivided by folding or sliding doors which would allow different activities to take place simultaneously. Smoking is not only a health hazard, it is an anti-social activity causing at best nuisance to many, at worst acute discomfort identified in tenants' responses as a reason for non-attendance.

Dividing doors and ventilators may be installed on existing schemes as well as in all new projects. Central location and covered access is an important factor influencing usage. Even very short distances deter people from using the facilities. At Bracknell, although common room and other communal facilities are centrally placed, some tenants whose terraced block faces away from the room, have to walk around the block to reach it. The evidence suggests that they were less inclined to use the facilities regularly on this account. Even within the scheme perceived inaccessibility by elderly people can provide a real disincentive to frequent use.

On the one scheme in which a dining room existed the amount of use did not seem to justify its inclusion on economic grounds alone, although there is daily usage by some who value the facility highly. Independence remains highly valued, not least by the elderly. They appear reluctant to trade-off the advantages of eating what and when they like, and with whom they like, for the convenience of meals centrally prepared at regular times. Given good health and a free choice, with a minimal financial penalty, most tenants opt for freedom of choice. This was especially marked among married couples. Predictably, many widows whilst they liked to eat with others, preferred to 'pop in and out' of friends and neighbours' houses for a cup of tea rather than elaborate patterns of dining together. Bracknell is the first of Hanover's schemes to provide a dining room, and the low level of use at the moment may not continue in the future or be paralleled on other schemes.

Our conclusion on the limited evidence available suggests the need for further experiments in providing community, self-catering facilities both to serve the scheme as a whole or on a more modest scale related to the common room. If grouped private bed-sitters were 'clustered', they might share common kitchen and dining areas.

Heating

The cost of heating was the single most important cause of dissatisfaction. Electric ceiling heating is both the least popular and the most expensive to the extent that it is not used by many people at all. We recommend the discontinuance of ceiling heating.(1) But further detailed study is required as to appropriate codes of practice so far as both heating and insulation are concerned. The general problem of escalating energy costs is now widely recognised and ways of economising in energy consumption within the home deserves the immediate attention of Hanover and indeed the building industry generally. This costs money and in any case requires design prototypes. Government will need to be responsive, both in supporting Hanover and others in the promotion of experimental schemes and in reviewing the financial arrangements and regulations which accompany support for such bodies, so that they continue to assist enterprise, initiative and innovation and do not become fetters on experiment and progress. Methods for more easy payment by installments for heating, and suggestions relating to advice and guidance on usage of different systems are discussed elsewhere.

Noise

Noise insulation is one of the issues which did not emerge as a significant problem in this study. Most of the people who were aware of noise were not bothered by it. Only in a few cases were external noises grounds for complaint and where noise through the night was a nuisance, the source was traffic and the schemes were those located near main roads, and in close proximity to town centres and related facilities. The dwellings generally provide reasonable standards of noise insulation. Noise from adjacent flats was generally caused by the volume at which radio and television was used or by people raising their voices due to deafness. Tenants rarely found this a nuisance. There was some evidence that these 'signs of life' were not unwelcome. They were perceived as a mixed blessing. The noises that did appear more annoying were those from wooden stairways and banging doors and lifts. Careful design and detailing with respect to the position, character and covering of stairways and common space could and generally does reduce this problem to minimal proportions.

Safety

The main concern with regard to alarm systems seemed to be the number of activation points that existed in the flat. People were concerned that they might fall some distance from the cord or button and be unable to reach the nearest one. The question of emergency calls is naturally important and any improvement in design which might help save lives must be considered. But there is a point beyond which it is no longer practicable or cost effective to design. The resources which would otherwise be deployed may be used to greater effect elsewhere. In short, improvements at the margin may only be secured at the risk of forfeiting opportunities elsewhere. Apart from the research which has been and is being done in this field, our own work indicates that Hanover have provided an adequate and trustworthy alarm call system. Many more activation points can be provided but the opportunity costs would be considerable and there is no evidence that this course of action would be worthwhile. But there are more modest improvements which could be made at minimum cost.

Often the alarm cord was mistaken for a light switch (especially by visitors, and children in particular) which could be prevented by using different colour cords, or buttons rather than cords.

The use of buttons seems a preferable alternative, perhaps at skirting board level with a protective cover over the point to avoid accidental activation. A further alternative which appeared to be successful in those schemes where it has already been installed, is the intercom system, allowing two-way conversation between warden and tenant.(2) Problems arose for the deaf who were unable to hear the warden clearly. The number of activation points remained a source of comment. But once the system had been explained adequately to tenants there was little dissatisfaction. One detail that requires improvement is the inadequacy of airing cupboards which were sometimes located near the front door backing on an external wall. Likewise, cold water pipe runs were sometimes taken through the cupboards which were inadequately insulated, resulting in difficulty in maintaining a temperature warm enough to effectively air clothes. Shelves were placed below rather than above the immersion heating. The result was that many tenants preferred to dry their clothes on top of or beside other heating facilities, which in the case of electric bar fires, presents a considerable fire hazard. A further problem in bathrooms which could easily be rectified relates to the design of grab poles, which in Bracknell in particular, tenants said became too slippery and dangerous to be of any use.

The use of non-slip covering material would enable a firm grip and decrease the possibility of a fall. Baths were sometimes said to be too deep, and tenants stated they had difficulty getting in and out of them. In some cases showers were suggested as an alternative and the suggestion made earlier about a free standing shower unit, perhaps adjacent to a guest room, might enable those tenants who preferred showers or who were perhaps temporarily or partially disabled to use one. Although Hanover's pre-occupation with the active elderly tends to preclude too much attention being given to the partially disabled, it may be wise to consider such facilities being installed in existing schemes and certainly the idea deserves exploration in new schemes.

To conclude, there is a high level of satisfaction in the safety aspects of flat design in Hanover's schemes and the specific issues raised are matters of design and detail that may relatively easily be rectified.

Windows

The study of Hanover schemes carried out by Mercer and Muir in 1967 showed that concern about windows was very common in the schemes they studied. This later study has not dealt in detail with window design, but when asked about possible design improvements tenants mentioned windows more than any other feature. The amount of light in halls was mentioned in Surbiton and ventilation was inadequate in the bathrooms of Royton and Cirencester. At Bracknell the flats on the upper storey of the terraced rows had no window in the front door and this also produced some comments about dark halls. Cleaning windows was difficult at Halifax where a large expanse of glass made it impossible to clean the outside from within the room, but the tenants in some cases commented that such a large window allowed them an unbroken view across the distant moors and valleys and so were able to see the advantages of this design. One possible solution to the problem of cleaning windows would be to organise cleaning services so that there would be no need for the elderly to risk accident by climbing onto furniture to clean their windows. But it is probable that a substantial number of people would still prefer to clean their own flats and would not wish nor be able to pay for such assistance.

In some cases the incorporation of a mechanical ventilator and/or a transom window would have been appreciated, to

109

allow better ventilation in kitchens and bathrooms. Mechanical ventilators had been installed sometimes especially in cases which had given rise to excessive condensation and this generally had improved matters.

The interaction between the high and increasing cost of energy, standards of thermal insulation, position, size and height of windows, airing cupboards, heating systems, washing appliances, and condensation, needs to be appreciated. If there is one area in which advances in building technology and systems design could have profoundly beneficial effects to the elderly, it is here. Not only because of the fixed and generally low incomes of this group, but because they feel the cold so. On the evidence of this study, the satisfaction with their homes would increase dramatically if we could do more in the interacting areas alluded to.

External design

As regards the privacy of schemes, 80 per cent of tenants interviewed expressed no dissatisfaction with the degree to which they were separated from the rest of the community. The setting and landscape requirements set down in Hanover's design requirements state that 'public footpaths are undesirable and where unavoidable should not be routed through the site but formed along the boundaries'. However, in the Bolton scheme, a well-used footpath (a long-standing right of way) which passes through the centre of the scheme and severs one block of flatlets from the other two, results in passers by and children causing considerable annoyance to some tenants. The problem is similar at Royton where a public footpath passes through the scheme and all tenants mentioned the use of the grounds as a public right of way and the presence of children. On other schemes without these problems there were occasional comments about the public use of car parking space within the scheme and the need to demarcate the boundary between public areas and private areas more clearly.

There were no schemes where problems of visual intrusion or overlooking from surrounding housing were mentioned. There was some desire expressed for gardens, especially on the Bracknell site and at Cirencester there were quite spacious garden plots which were well managed, but generally tenants seemed content with the facilities which were provided, even if only a small window garden.

LOCATIONAL REQUIREMENTS

Hanover's site requirements to architects state that 'schemes should be normally within a quarter of a mile of shops, a regular bus route, post office, church and a pub'. The schemes selected in this study have demonstrated that these objectives have generally been achieved and that most tenants interviewed were satisfied with the location of their scheme. The suggestion that a chemist be included in the list would predictably be greeted with the unanimous assent of tenants on several schemes not so well served in this respect. Likewise a post office was sometimes further away than many tenants liked or felt able to walk. These specific examples apart, most tenants were able to reach all the facilities and amenities they required, and usually on foot.

Shopping is the most frequent activity involving travel and Hanover has been successful in providing a wide range of choice in most cases.

Where schemes were not situated in or very near to the town centre itself, there were usually alternative shopping facilities available within 10 minutes' walking distance at which most daily needs could be met. Even where this was the case many tenants, especially the more active, preferred to walk to the town centre anyway. Obviously the town centre has an attraction which extends beyond the purely practical one of being a place to shop. Many people liked to walk or catch a bus to the centre to simply walk around and watch and be part of the activity there. The ease with which this kind of activity could be carried out was greatly appreciated by those tenants in easily accessible schemes.

The factors which affect a 'satisfactory' location are extremely diverse and are only now being investigated in any depth. Current research is concentrating on the mobility of the elderly, their travel patterns and use of facilities (shopping in particular) (Hillman, 1973). Other aspects

111

relevant to location are also under investigation, like the safety of the elderly from traffic.

However, this information has not been drawn together and related to the locational requirements of sheltered, or any other form of housing scheme for the elderly. Of particular importance is the relative importance of different facilities to the typical scheme population, so that explicit trade offs can be made in selection of sites.

We need to know how people value these aspects of schemes and to what extent they will choose one against another. There has been a lot of question-begging in the past and assumptions about preferences have been used as the basis for policy, without clear investigations of 'consumer' attitudes. The aim of such work would be to establish more specific locational criteria, which would include environmental aspects like noise and topography as well as the social aspects referred to above (characteristics of neighbourhood, likelihood of intrusion).

There will never be a location which will satisfy all tenants at all times; however, it is probable that a central location would allow greater independence to a larger number of tenants than an isolated 'green field site. Not only are shopping facilities more easily accessible, but library, theatre, cinema activities are usually available. As well as this, the transport system is likely to be more regular, comprehensive and cheaper; (concessionary fares are more often available in urban than rural areas) and welfare services closer at hand. This last point is significant when projecting the role of the sheltered housing movement into the future. If the present climate of opinion continues there will be an increasing desire to move away from the concept of the institutional residential home and towards the grouped housing concept with its offer of greater independence for its tenants, and a situation in which tenants can continue their former life style as nearly as possible. If desirable social and health objectives are to minimise the incidence and extent of uprooting old people and to encourage even the partially disabled and very old to retain their independence to remain in one scheme for as long as possible, then the presence of domiciliary welfare services will increase the possibility of that happening. It is not presently one of the functions of the warden to care for increasingly disabled tenants, but the number of people in this category will increase dramatically in the next ten years. The more convenient and comprehensive the welfare service available close at hand, the less likely it is that tenants will be forced to move from one type of accommodation to another as their needs alter over time. The locational issues for Hanover and for the agencies working in this field have much greater importance when considered in this broader way against a social, economic and environmental context that is radically different from what it was - a gap that is widening rather than narrowing.

Finally, highly valued urban land offering pedestrians maximum accessibility to the widest range of facilities may provide the most desirable location for old people's dwellings. Many authorities, including Birmingham, would encourage provision of housing for the elderly in such locations and the central area has its attractions for the old as well as the young. The air space above existing or proposed commercial development would be relatively inexpensive and in some cases might be provided free of cost to an association such as Hanover.

LOCAL MANAGEMENT

The warden's role and space implications

There is a need for further study of the role of wardens and the attitudes not only of the wardens themselves, but of tenants, tenants' relatives and the officials of local authorities which are often ambiguous and contradictory. The concept of a resident warden who is more than a landlady, but less than a hospital nurse, is highly relevant. As we have indicated many wardens are dissatisfied with the degree of privacy currently afforded and we have referred to the design and spatial implications earlier. Likewise, there is a need to consider different mixes of dwellings by size and living arrangements. It may be socially acceptable and economically desirable to provide shared accommodation for groups of elderly willing to accept the advantages which such groupings might also bring with it.

Contact between wardens could be improved with advantage. Exchanges of views, especially for the newly appointed warden, would be invaluable. Subsequent and regular informal contact between wardens would provide the opportunity to air views and discuss problems, gaining from the experience and advice of others working in Hanover and other housing associations. This view has been expressed in general terms at the formal meetings that are arranged for wardens. A National Association for Wardens has been suggested by an Age Concern Working Party and the movement toward professional status for wardens which could lead to a standardisation of pay, conditions, and grades of responsibility, appears to be gaining momentum.

Contact between warden and tenant

As well as contact between the wardens themselves, there is a greater need for contact between prospective tenant and warden. The value of warden-tenant committees is often underestimated and will become more important and necessary in the future. Elderly parents often move home from one end of the country to the other to be nearer their children or other relatives, and the flat is found for them by their relatives and everything arranged in their absence. There were cases where tenants said that if they had seen the scheme, the town or the flat first, they would either have looked for another to become available, or not moved at all. The relatively simple procedure of encouraging the prospective tenant to come to talk to the warden and walk round the scheme, to see for themselves the facilities available (there were also cases of expectations about facilities not being fulfilled) would prevent disappointment and subsequent dissatisfaction. Once tenants have become installed in the flat, and taking into account the fact that it will often be the first time they have lived in a home with central heating, advice and guidance from the appropriate authority on how best to operate the system could save a great deal of time and money. Written instructions are often not understood and the best approach is sympathetic and appropriate guidance from an authority official.

Safety and fire precautions

A similar procedural point relates to the essential role of wardens' and tenants' committee in relation to safety precautions, within the dwelling and the scheme as a whole. We have no doubt that the real fears expressed by some tenants and wardens, at, what they consider to be inadequate fire precautions and equipment require investigation. It is likewise essential that periodic checks are carried out of equipment and highly desirable that fire-prevention officers meet tenants as well as wardens - it is not a statutory requirement - to explain the measures taken for their safety, answer questions and demonstrate the use of hydrants and extinguisheers, etc. (3)

Payment for heating

Payment for heating is a procedural issue also requiring co-operation between local authorities and a shift in policy which could affect an area of considerable sensitivity. It was apparent that payment in a quarterly lump sum, which in some cases amounted to over £60, meant that tenants were deterred from using their main heating systems, and often relied on supplementary heaters provided in the flat, or their own portable heaters.

Payment of heating bills on a monthly basis together with the rent, would be preferred, although because of rent legislation affecting housing associations, this raises practical difficulties in that increases in costs cannot necessarily be recovered.

Communications

On any scheme, however well-organised and however well tenants operate the facilities available, there will always be repairs necessary and grievances to discuss. Communal facilities will be more or less popular according to tenant characteristics, facilities in the area and factors intrinsic to particular schemes. Problems will arise when tenants become disabled, require extra welfare services, and are dissatisfied with or are unable to obtain, those that do exist. These kinds of problems are the sort that Hanover itself needs to know about, i.e specifically 'internal' problems, perhaps of design, or procedure, which provide a constant feedback about the effectiveness of schemes and which hopefully enable improvements by being fed into an ongoing design process. For this reason, more explicit recognition of the importance of communication, both formal and informal, is necessary. The warden plays the key role in all this, being at the centre, hopefully, of all relevant information channels. The warden also provides the link between tenant and Hanover. She exercises considerable power measured in residents' satisfaction or the converse. She is privy to information about tenants' problems and internal aspects of schemes and to information involving the gas, electricity, water boards and other authorities engaged in servicing the site as well as social services. The warden has a unique opportunity to co-ordinate efforts from many directions.

Warden-tenant committees

The importance of the need to improve contact between wardens and wardens and tenants has been stressed already. Finally, although the survey raised many questions, the value of tenant committees working with and assisting the warden was perhaps underestimated. The importance of participation in the affairs of any schemes is likely to grow in importance. Informal association and contact appears to be successful in Hanover's schemes and this may in part be due to the wardens' qualities and in part to the relatively small size of schemes. In larger schemes, more things go wrong and lines of communication can become stretched. Closer working relationships through warden-tenant committees should be fostered and supported if tenants feel this would be helpful.

GENERAL POLICY

Dimensions of change

In this section we examine some of the dimensions of change in the wider policy environment which could have important implications for Hanover and other housing associations; critical longer term issues which have an important bearing on the whole concept of sheltered housing and the role it will

116

play in the future.

Demographic, economic and social change is having a decisive influence on the direction which housing provision for the aged is likely to take over the next ten to fifteen years. Already there are considerable shifts in attitude and interest. For example, in the role the warden may and will be expected to play, in the scope of sheltered housing schemes and the relationships between them and the social services departments of local authorities. Discussion has underlined the overwhelming desire of elderly people to remain independent for as long as possible. In the United States, many condominium schemes for old people include for the necessary supportive facilities to be available on site, including the inevitable home with nursing care for those becoming progressively incapacitated for one reason or another. These schemes mostly fall within the private sector and they demonstrate the preferences of those with the necessary resources. But the response of voluntary organisations, religious and charitable foundations, suggests that this type of provision commands considerable support.

Because the trend towards greater independence and self-help is likely to continue, the character, component parts and scale of sheltered housing schemes are likely to change substantially in the next decade.

The provision of flatlets, incorporating design specifications which enable a heterogeneous tenant community might well become a model or ideal to strive for. The reduced necessity for moving would be beneficial to large numbers of old people who become increasingly frail and partially disabled. The possibility of staying at home or within the same group, and of being supported even when suffering from illness could alleviate the negative psychological consequences which often accompany the onset of partial mobility and other ailments associated with advancing years. This is not to say that the wardens will become nurses as their tenant population grows older - this could obviously not be expected or desired. Although the warden's role will come to be seen as increasingly important, as co-ordinator of various agents, and agencies, it is the domiciliary services themselves which will bear the brunt.

117

Questions of co-ordination with the supporting services and their relationship with the warden and the housing association will take on a greater importance and are linked with another area of future development which we feel will influence and be influenced by these choices; this is the pronounced shift in emphasis towards conversion as a means of improving the supply of sheltered housing and making the best use of existing resources, both existing housing stock and ancillary facilities.

The costs and benefits of conversion

The trend in sheltered housing has been towards new building, but problems of cost and site availability have made this reappraisal of conversion an attractive additional alternative. Such a policy has the apparent advantage of locating existing converted housing close to necessary facilities and services at a lower cost than new building. A possible method of carrying out such research using existing design criteria might be:

(i)   Cost of converting properties to a suitable standard - compare resulting life of property, running costs, development time, standard and conversion costs with equivalent sized new development. The range of sizes relating to cost effectiveness and satisfaction is relevant in this connection not least because of the increased reliance on supportive care to retain the independence of the elderly at home. Location of other health facilities is becoming an established factor in the situation.

(ii) Cost and availability of suitable properties in different urban situations compared with sites for new development.

(iii) Other possible benefits or costs of conversions, e.g. in terms of relative location, finished appearance, etc.

(iv) Use survey techniques to establish tenants' reactions to conversions compared with new developments.

Difficulty in this will be in matching, or controlling for the many variations between the different types of scheme. One of the undoubted problems of conversion relates to potential fire hazard, meeting the various building regulations, etc. Conversion in this sense is never administratively or organisationally a 'soft option'. Yet in the wider context of securing advantages of accessibility and conservation of scarce resources, the potential gains may well appear worth investigating in more detail than hitherto. In many medium and small towns, where from the analysis of mobility trends many people would like to live, and indeed to which many old people are moving, there is residential property which is accessible on foot to a wide range of those very facilities which are essential for the well-being, satisfaction and independence of elderly people. Such property is often relatively cheap compared with prices elsewhere in the cities. Likewise, such smaller towns have not the range of problems that inner areas of many of our larger cities have. They are better able to cater for the needs of a section of the population that is no longer productive.

Provision of communal facilities in sheltered housing

At the present the provision of communal facilities in sheltered housing is not based on any sound set of social or planning criteria. It is a relatively arbitrary and intuitive affair and it is not altogether surprising that there is plenty of evidence pointing to considerable under use of some existing facilities in certain cases and of heavy demand for missing facilities in others. One critical issue upon which the extent of provision, particularly rooms, must depend is the intended role of the sheltered housing scheme, e.g. the intended degree of independence the elderly should retain. Other factors which ought to be taken into account are the provision of alternative facilities in the immediate neighbourhood, the ownership rates by tenants of washing machines, driers, etc., the preferences of the tenants (e.g. whether they would wish to use common facilities or not) and the cost of providing such facilities and equipping them.

What attitudinal studies of the kind discussed here do not do is assess the preferences <u>between</u> facilities where such a choice has to be made in conditions of economic and financial stringency.

A possible method of examining these important questions might be:-

(i)   select schemes which contain the facilities and measure the relevant variables to relate to the use of the facilities; also obtain residents' attitudes

(ii)   select schemes without facilities and investigate tenants' adaptive behaviour in absence of facilities, plus their attitudes (e.g. how much they would pay to use facilities)

(iii)   find schemes where facilities have been added or removed and look at any changes in behaviour/attitude resulting from the change.

The location of sheltered housing

Current research is concentrating on the mobility of the elderly, their travel patterns, and use of facilities (shopping in particular). Other aspects relevant to location are also under investigation, e.g. safety of the elderly from traffic. However, this information has not yet been drawn together and related to the locational attributes of a sheltered housing scheme. The locational attributes of Hanover's schemes are varied if not arbitrary. The locational pattern reflects the history of the Association; what it has and has not been able to do. The provision of sites reflects the good will of a variety of agencies whether civic or ecclesiastical. What seems likely is that there will be advantages, both social and economic, in giving greater importance to this factor than ever before. Of particular importance is the relative attraction of different facilities to the typical scheme population, so that explicit trade-offs can be made in selection of sites.

Further study might be carried out in two stages. Firstly, making use of existing and further work to identify the locational needs and preferences of various socio-economic groups with respect to sheltered housing. This might take into account, for example, the trade-off between the high quality bed-sit accommodation, shared group communal facilities, high levels of insulation, immediate access on foot to town centre shopping and amenities and more conventional 'green fields' cottage type development. Secondly, the relevance of factors such as partial disability and the location of relevant social services to decisions on whether to provide more sheltered housing. It must be recognised that the growing concentrations of older people in certain areas might have serious social and economic consequences over the longer term. Further study on the distribution of the aged population is relevant to location policy.

It has been correctly suggested that the differences in institutions and administrative practice between the UK and, for example, the US or other countries in Europe needs to be explicitly recognised in any cross-cultural comparisons. The brief references to Dutch and American policy and practice illustrates the potential value of a comparative study of policy and practice in housing for the aged within the European Community and the United States. The first stage of such a study would no doubt examine the standards adopted within each country and the relative importance attached to various categories of dwellings and relevant regulations.

A specific review of Hanover's Notes for Guidance has not been undertaken as an explicit part of this study. It is recommended that they be reviewed and systematised in the light of this study. Before being finalised they might usefully be issued as a consultative document to architects who have designed schemes for Hanover and to a sample of wardens. Such a specific review of Hanover design practice would result in a much more detailed and useful design manual. Whilst such design manuals and codes of practice cannot guarantee good design, they can indicate clearly what is expected by the client.

Experimental schemes

But perhaps the key to practical progress in the next few years lies in a series of specific experimental schemes, or schemes only aspects of which are experimental. Such

121

schemes, or part schemes, would be built explicitly to meet a variety of objectives. It would be the task of continuous policy review and design evaluation to assess the effectiveness of such schemes over time in meeting these objectives and to produce information on both behaviour and attitudes of tenants, and the costs and benefits of alternative ways of attempting to achieve objectives.

The only, or almost only, effective strategy for improving performance in this area must be by creating an experiment that can be observed. It is true of course that this may well be costly, but except where simulation techniques allow reasonable prediction of the performance of physical solutions or allow measurement of environmental impacts and nuisances, we have to rely on manipulating physical design variables, i.e. aspects of the man-made environment and assessing the behavioural and attitudinal implications of such manipulation on various sections of the population, broken down into categories such as the elderly for relevant purposes.

There are many proposals for experimental schemes which deserve most careful consideration. Some are complex in that they go beyond physical design and require system design skills and the introduction of new social networks involving a variety of institutions including government. Others are relatively simple and could be implemented more easily by an Association such as Hanover.

Proposals which might be considered include those concerned with:-

(i)   Greater variations in dwelling sizes and methods of grouping dwellings within schemes; specifically the introduction of more bedsitters together with increased provision of shared facilities by groups and increased provision of community facilities for the scheme as a whole.

        There is a need to extend the range of facilities, to extend choice, to help the aged to live independently. There is a need for more single storey dwellings which avoid any stairs and with good planning, both

122

thermal and sound insulation can be improved. Clustered single storey dwellings are capable of maximum flexibility as to size and numbers of bedrooms. Internal staircases are to be avoided and only increase hazards within the home and add to the circulation space and household chores.

(ii)   Greater variation in size of schemes and categories of old persons' dwelling. If additional facilities to serve the partially disabled and the sick are required within the scheme, then the optimum size may well be very different from those currently provided by associations for the 'active elderly'.

A greater variation and degree of internal flexibility in dwelling size would be advantageous. More specifically, an increase in bed-sitters could be combined with improved communal facilities and higher levels of thermal insulation. Tenants' preferences to experimental schemes where there was an explicit trade-off in private space for improved heating at lower running costs for greater public space would be valuable. Such a policy would probably result in a higher level of usage for any guest rooms or ground floor flat for the disabled, or associated facilities including a shower unit, provided.

Arguably, the size of such a scheme might be larger than hitherto, with office and managerial functions being adequately catered for in terms of space and equipment.

A variant of this recommendation would be to specifically include facilities for shared accommodation by three and four persons; such a group would require in addition to a bed-sitter private room, a lounge, and an additional small bedroom though perhaps the bedroom could be a shared facility with the next door group of residents.

(iii) Taking advantage of air space in central areas or in district shopping centres of cities and towns. Many

123

local authorities may provide free sites above ground or first floor level, above shopping and commercial activities which only require low level accommodation. Many private developers may be willing to incorporate such facilities as part of a negotiated development with the local planning authority, especially where the land is owned by the community.

One of the most interesting experiments, especially suitable for central or inner city areas where such schemes would be useful, would be the provision of service flats with the provision of domestic help, communal facilities and services including hot meals. Such a combination of support for the aged could be provided most appropriately in high density areas, ideally located near to neighbourhood social services. Such schemes would no doubt be larger than those examined in this study. No doubt such schemes would be preferred by those who are less mobile and afflicted by some disability. Such a scheme would require a warden with clearly specified duties, whilst opportunities would be created for providing a variety of communal facilities within the scheme itself. If the elderly have all support facilities and easy access to facilities, then there may be advantages in providing bed-sit accommodation; certainly advantages derived from possibilities of introducing a variety of dwelling sizes could be gained from such an approach. Arguably, such a scheme could provide central accommodation at relatively modest rental values. Finally, if air space could be provided for such accommodation, the high cost of land could be avoided.

(iv)   Improved thermal and acoustic insulation; integrated technical systems designed to conserve energy.

(v)   Conversion of existing accommodation of varying characteristics on appropriately located sites in the arcadian middle ring of cities.

(vi)   More controlled experiments in the provision and use

124

of communal space, both inside and outside the building.

(vii) Experimental design of wardens' accommodation and office. It may be related to the provision of a flat and shower unit suitable for those partially disabled and temporarily ill.

(viii) Relationships between sheltered housing and other service and care facilities on the same or nearby sites.

There would be advantages in relating several experimental and even traditional schemes to a service home. In Holland, complete intra mural care is provided for the aged who live in apartments in service homes. There is a maximum of three staff for every ten residents. The apartments are designed for single persons or couples. The service home also has communal facilities. There is often a sick bay for short term cases and sometimes an intensive care section, both of limited capacity. The capacity of homes being projected currently varies from 60 to 200 places. The optimum capacity is stated to be between 80 and 120 places. About three quarters of the residents receive financial support through the National Assistance Act. (4)

(ix) Relationships between sheltered housing and tailored adaptions of normal (family-type) houses to suit the partially disabled or the less mobile.

(x) The provision of service flats in central areas together with combined support facilities.

The emphasis on co-ordination is important. The design of social systems is both necessary and difficult and only by a functional approach to organisation and management is progress likely to be made in this field. The Dutch experience is relevant. There are four ministries, Housing and Physical Planning, Cultural Affairs, Recreation and Social Work; Health and Environmental Hygiene; and Social

125

Affairs, whose efforts are co-ordinated through the Interdepartmental Steering Committee for Policy Relating to the Care of the Aged. The numerous private organisations have an umbrella organisation in the Netherlands Federation for Policy Relating to the Care of the Aged, which represents their interests to Central Government. The philosophy and practice of member countries in the European Economic Community deserves much closer comparative study. This constitutes a valuable area for further research, especially in considering the extent to which basic physiological and psychological aspects are treated similarly and the extent to which standards differ and reflect economic, social and cultural differences.

There would be advantages in Hanover Housing Association together with an appropriate research and development team, and a firm specialising in thermal insulation applications and/or window design, collaborating in an experimental scheme or schemes which seek to compare traditional practice with applications designed to cut down on noise transmission and improve on thermal standards of insulation.

It would be essential to compare like with like, both for physical performance, social impact and costs. The philosophical basis for this work is that monitoring of physical performance and behavioural response is built into the exercise so that the costs and benefits associated with building innovation may be evaluated within some acceptable calculus. Such an approach accepts the need for a range of controlled experiments, build, monitor, analyse and build again.

Such an approach (5) is adopted in a prototype group of solar homes for the elderly due to begin in September 1976 at Bebington, Merseyside, designed by Peter Greenwood, Director of Building Sciences, Institute of Advanced Architectural Studies,

126

University of York, and Dr. Howard Ward, Head of Construction Studies, Plymouth Polytechnic. The essence of this scheme is energy conservation. It uses only one fifth of the total energy used by an average well insulated house:

"'a house needs energy for temperature control, hot water, lighting, and small power and cooking. Of these, the greatest energy demand is probably on temperature control within the house by controlling the movement of heat through the outer shell.'"

In this dwelling, windows, and doors have also been carefully considered with <u>double</u> double glazing in windows and two entrance doors in place of one. Detailed specifications of such an experimental scheme would have to be worked out.

The approach which needs to be incorporated in the detailed design brief, probably after a series of discussions with the principals involved is that of <u>integrated environmental design</u> in providing an economical solution for the provision of space heating and hot water that can be applied at minimal running costs in old peoples' housing and with minimum attention required from the old people themselves. Total costs rather than first costs must be considered in any economic analysis. Perceptions of efficiency must relate to old people themselves.(6)

It will be evident from the foregoing that the study has persuaded us of the value of building schemes which explore overall concepts of an old person's dwelling and its relationship not simply to family housing and social amenities, but to the housing group of which it forms a part. Some of these ideas will require further study before a sound and cost-effective brief emerges.

Procedural and administrative aspects

Where relaxation or waivers are required from government to allow such experiments to carry the necessary degree of financial support, this should not unreasonably be witheld. An experimental category of scheme to be the subject of study should be introduced into this growing and critical field. Indeed, such an approach would reveal the procedural, organisational, legal and other institutional difficulties which may need critical study and lead to administrative and financial adjustments in current categorisation by the Department of what schemes and facilities are, and are not, eligible for grant. In an important sense, procedural adjustments and decision rules for grant are interactive with the results of an experimental building programme. A comprehensive review of procedures and administrative aspects relating to sheltered housing might constitute a complementary component of such a programme. What is suggested is the establishment of a continuous review process of policy formulation, implementation and evaluation related to categories of sheltered housing confined to the type represented by Hanover and concentrating on new experiments and ideas.

NOTES

1. This form of heating has, in fact, been discontinued as previously indicated.
2. Since 1976, the provision of speech-call systems has been standard practice.
3. Action has been taken as indicated in note 3, Chapter 2
4. 'Special Housing Needs in the Netherlands', Ministry of Housing and Physical Planning, The Hague, 1976
5. RIBAJ, November 1976
6. Another example of an experimental scheme relates to the Energy Conservation House, Machynlleth, North Wales, Architects Peter Bond and Associates, Wates Built Homes, Ltd., Contractors

Appendices

PART I

Appendix I: Twenty-five Selected Tables Derived from Questionnaire Surveys

Appendix II: Hanover Housing Association and the Voluntary Housing Movement

Appendix III: The Questionnaires - an explanatory note

Appendix IV: Hanover Housing Association - terms of reference

APPENDIX I

Twenty-five selected tables derived from questionnaire surveys

Table 1

Ten Selected Schemes: Location, Age, Unit Size, Number of Beds/Tenants, Distance from Town Centre, Communal Facilities

Area	Scheme	Date	No/Type Unit	No. Tenants	Distance* (miles)	Communal Facilities
South West	Cheltenham	1968	41 (BS, SB, DB)	41	1.5	Common/drying room
	Cirencester	1973	30 (SB)	40	0.3	Hobbies/guest room, laundry
	Tewkesbury	1972	29 (DB)	36	0.1	Drying room
North West	Bolton	1971	29 (SB)	37	2.0	No communal facilities
	Halifax	1971	57 (DB)	72	1.5	Guest/common room
	Oldham	1973	26 (DB)	31	0.5	Drying room
	Royton	1975	31 (DB)	39	0.1	Guest room/laundry
South	Bracknell	1974	41 (DB, 2B)	52	2.0	Guest room/common room/laundry
	Caversham	1972	21 (DB)	25	4.0	Guest room
	Surbiton	1969	26 (SB, DB)	28	0.1	Common/drying room

Key
BS - Bedsitter
SB - Single bedroom (minimum area of $6.5m^2$; minimum width 1.83m)
DB - Double bedroom (minimum area of $12.5m^2$; minimum width 2.6m)

Table 2

Ten Selected Schemes: Number of Tenants, Number of Completed Interviews, Sample Characteristics of each Scheme

Scheme	Tenants on Scheme	Interviews Completed	Scheme % Female	Scheme % Single Widow	Sample % Female	Sample % Single Widow
Bolton	37	15	75.7	56.7	80.0	73.3
Bracknell	52	21	73.1	53.8	66.7	52.4
Caversham	25	11	68.0	60.0	81.8	63.6
Cheltenham	41	18	92.7	95.1	94.4	94.4
Cirencester	40	15	72.5	55.0	66.7	46.7
Halifax	72	29	80.4	59.7	86.2	75.9
Oldham	31	13	77.4	67.7	84.6	69.2
Royton	39	15	71.8	59.0	73.3	73.3
Surbiton	28	13	78.8	69.7	92.3	84.6
Tewkesbury	36	14	72.2	44.4	78.6	64.3
Total	401	164				

Table 3

Ten Selected Schemes: Age, Ambulatory, Length of Residence, Characteristics, by Tenants Interviewed for each Scheme

Scheme	Tenants Interviewed	Average Age	Tenants over 70 %	Tenants over 80 %	Sample ambulant %	Date of Scheme	Average Length of Residence (years)
Bolton	15	71.8	53.3	13.3	93.3	1971	3.5
Bracknell	21	71.0	57.1	-	100.0	1974	1.5
Caversham	11	74.8	77.7	33.3	72.7	1972	3.5
Cheltenham	18	74.8	77.7	11.1	94.4	1968	6.1
Cirencester	15	72.6	66.7	-	86.7	1973	3.1
Halifax	29	72.8*	-	-	93.1	1971	2.7
Oldham	13	70.5*	-	-	100.0	1973	2.3
Royton	15	70.1*	-	-	100.0	1975	0.7
Surbiton	13	76.6	76.9	15.4	100.0	1969	5.3
Tewkewbury	14	73.0	58.4	16.7	85.7	1972	2.8
Total	164						

* Based on estimates of tenants' ages only

Table 4

Ten Selected Schemes: Characteristics Liked by Tenants

Scheme		Ratio of likes to dislikes
Bolton	Quiet (4); Compact, size of flat (4); Well designed, convenience (2); Heating good/warm (2); Warm (2); Helpful warden (1); Easy to keep clean (1); No vandalism (1); Good kitchen (1)	1:00
Bracknell	View/outlook (2); Like living upstairs (2); Warden's presence (1); Quiet (1); Bus cheap (1); Satisfied (1); Age Concern help good (1)	0:43
Caversham Park	Easy to run/clean (2); New friends/relatives (2); Heating/hot water good (2); View/outlook (1); Modern facilities (1); No garden (1); Convenient to shops (1); Rent reasonable (1); Hand rails (1); Spacious (1); Right number of people (1)	0:88
Cheltenham	Good gardens (5); Well designed (4); Size of rooms, compact (4); View/outlook (3); Location in town (3); Comfortable (2); Heating good (2); Nice old house (1); Modern amenities (1); Friendly (1); Near relatives (1); Private (1); Quiet (1); Like living upstairs (1); Easy to run (1); Self-contained, but near other people (1); Good outside lighting (1)	1:57
Cirencester	Compact, size of rooms/flat (5); Well designed for elderly, safety (4); Community Spirit/nice people (3); Easy to run/clean (2); Good kitchen separate (2); Good gardens (1); Warden's presence (1); Satisifed (1); Nice layout of flats (1); Level - no stairs (1); Convenient for shops (1); Situation good (1); Separated from young people (1); End flat - more windows (1); Large windows (1); Scheme a good idea (1); Spare cupboard useful (1); Good view/outlook (2)	1:03
Halifax	View/outlook (8); Easy to run/clean (3); Good layout of flats (3); Satisfied (2); Nice flat (2); Level - no stairs (2); Quiet (1); Warden's presence (1); Pleasant (1); End flat - more windows (1); Lounge (1); Bedroom (1); Telephone (1); Home area (1); People mind thier own business (1)	0:63
Oldham	Satisfied (2); Nice flat (2); Airiness/sunlight (2); View/outlook (1); Modern amenities (1); Comfortable (1); Private (1); Everything (1); Good outside lighting (1); Heating good (1); Nice layout of flat (1); Level - no stairs (1); Pleasant (1); Bathroom (1)	0:77
Royton	Nice flat (2); View/outlook (1); Easy to run/clean (1); Convenient to shops (1); Windows easy to clean (1); Near buses (1)	0:30
Surbiton	Good neighbourhood (2); View/outlook (1)	0:30
Tewkesbury	Location in town (9); View/outlook (7); Size of rooms/flat, compact (7); Warden's presence, Well designed (2); Friendly (1); Private (1)	1:08

137

Table 5

Ten Selected Schemes: Characteristics Disliked by Tenants

Scheme	
Bolton	Drying problems (3); Heating expensive (2); Windows poor (2); Would prefer ground floor (2); High rent/rates (1); Lonely (1); Steps (1); Would like second bedroom (1); No privacy (1); Intrusion (1); Rubbish in grounds (1)
Bracknell	Heating expensive (4); Too near other housing, etc. (2); Poor storage heaters (2); No shops (1); High rent/rates (1); Poor view (1); Poor construction (1); Immersion heater (1); Prefer central heating (1); Kitchen dark (1)
Caversham Park	High rent/rates (1); Rubbish bins (1); Flooding (1); Noisy (1); Intrusion (1); Poor hand rails (1); Damp site (1); Near footpath (1); Heating poor (1); Doors draughty (1); Cupboard high/low (2); Doors hit (1); Poor grab pole location (1); Insects (1); Drying problem (1)
Cheltenham	Want separate kitchen (2); Long way to shops (1) Prefer own toilet (1); More cupboard room needed (1); Noisy lift (1); Emergency cord (1); Heavy traffic (1); Cleaning of communal areas (1); Access to Hanover (1); Doors banging (1); Poor maintenance (1); Windows difficult to clean (1); Heating expensive (1); High rent/rates (1); Refuse bins (1); Damp (1); Lift bumpy (1); Don't like filling heater (1); Complaints not dealt with confidentially (1); Poor view (1)
Cirencester	Heating expensive (6); Poor finish (4); Bedroom too small (3); No windows in bathrooms (3); High rent/rates (1); Poor view (1); Noisy (1); Cupboards (1); Weeds in garden (1); Slow completion work (1); Bathroom heater and light on same switch (1); Flat for disabled hard to alter (1); Deputy Alarm system (1); No alternative heating type (1); Kitchen design (1); Not enough storage (1); Ceiling heating no good (1)
Halifax	Poor view (5); Windows poor (4); Site unattractive (3); More cupboard room needed (3); Windows difficult to clean (2); High rent/rates (2); Noisy (2); Drying difficult (2); Cupboards low/high (2); Insects (2); Need more power points (2); Flooding (2); Cold (1); Heating inadequate (1); Door draughty (1); Noisy lift (1); Hanover maintenance poor (1); Too small (1); Poor construction (1); Weeds in garden (1); No windows in bathroom (1); Ceiling heating no good (1); Floors (1); Cracks in ceiling (1)
Oldham	Hot water slow to heat (4); Poor security (3); Poor lighting (2); Noisy (2); Poor layout (1); Shut off from everything (1); Drying room upstairs (1); Poorly positioned light switches (1); Damp in kitchen (1); Long way to shops (1); Windows - difficult to clean (1); Heating expensive (1); High rent/rates (1); Poor view (1); External Noise (1)
Royton	Immersion heater (3); No windows in bathroom (3); Heating off in summer (3); Children (2); Drying problems (2); High rent/rates (1); Refuse bins (1); Fitted heating not liked (1); Poor view (1); Too near other housing (1); Garden difficult to reach (1); No privacy (1); Intrusion (1); Cracks in walls (1); Warden does not clean place (1)
Surbiton	Windows difficult to clean (2); Windows poor (2); Windows difficult to reach (2); Poor view (1); Poor lighting (1); Damp in kitchen (1); Lights out at 11.30 p.m. (1)
Tewkesbury	Poor construction (5); Entrance shabby (3); Heavy traffic (2); Poor finish (2); Too small (1); External noise (1); Light bulbs difficult to change (1); Immersion heater (1); Bath too small (1); No communal life (1)

Table 6

Persons Using Additional Heating

Heating System	No. of tenants	% of tenants	Reasons Given (No. of tenants giving reason)
Gas warm air	10	77	Occasional supplement (5) Cold at times in certain rooms (4) Dislike gas (1)
Electric underfloor and ceiling	19	79	When it is very cold (8) Before heating comes on in evening (2) Too expensive (8) Occasional supplement (5) Main heating insufficient (3) Do not like ceiling heating (3) In cold weather (2) For visual focus (2)
Gas central heating	8	53	In summer when heating off (7) Occasional supplement (1)
Electric storage	60	72	In very cold weather (21) Storage inadequate (14) Before storage comes on evening (12) Occasional supplement (5) Visual attraction (2) Drying washing (1) Dislike storage (1)

Table 7

Persons not Using Main Heating System

Heating system	No. of tenants	% of tenants with heating	Reason Given (No. of tenants giving reason)
Gas warm air	1	8	Do not like gas (1)
Electric underfloor	-	-	-
Electric ceiling	18	72	Too expensive (7) Not sufficient (5) Not cold enough yet (2) Alternative heating sufficient (2) Too stuffy (1) Cracks ceiling (1)
Gas central heating	-	-	-
Electric storage	1	1	Too stuffy (1)

N.B. Four tenants (5 per cent) said that they did not use the electric storage heaters provided in all rooms

140

Table 8

Quarterly Heating Costs in All Schemes

No. of Tenants saying:	Quarterly Heating Costs in All Schemes								
	Under £10	£10-£19.99	£20-£29.99	£30-£39.99	£40-£49.99	£50-£59.99	£60-£69.99	£70-£79.99	Over £80
Heating more expensive than normal	-	1+4*	3+3*	6	14	16	8	3	2
Heating not more expensive than normal	2*	2+2*	3+5*	16	13	13	3	1	-
Total	2*	3+6*	6+8*	22	27	29	11	4	2

* Refers to tenants with gas heating systems; all other costs are inclusive of cooking, lighting, etc.

Table 9

Satisfaction with Different Heating Systems

Heating System	Number of Tenants	Average Heating Satisfaction	% of Tenants not Warm Enough (main heating only)	
			Day	Night
Gas warm air	13	3.4	7	7
Electric underfloor	24	3.6	38	25
Electric ceiling	26	2.6	19	23
Gas central heating	15	4.3	-	-
Electric storage	86	3.8	20	18

142

Table 10	
Internal Safety, Design Alterations suggested by Tenants	
Comment/Suggested Change of Flat Design for Safety	Times Mentioned
Windows difficult to clean	10
Lower cupboards better	9
Bath/bath pole slippery	8
Bath too small	4
Shower instead of bath	4
No fire escape/need fire door	3
Lighter corridors required	3
Grab pole in bathroom/toilet poorly based	3
Light outside alley/external lighting	3
Ceiling/curtains too high	2
Cupboards too low	2
Need additional alarm cord	2
Need security intercom	2
Better switch to plug position required	2
Doors hard to operate	2

Table 11

Ten Selected Schemes: Noise Nuisance - Percentage of Tenants Affected by Noise or Neighbours' T.V.

Scheme	Noise	T.V.
Bolton	20.0%	-
Bracknell	29.0%	5.0%
Caversham Park	18.0%	36.0%
Cheltenham	28.0%	39.0%
Cirencester	20.0%	47.0%
Halifax	24.0%	28.0%
Oldham	23.0%	23.0%
Royton	27.0%	33.0%
Surbiton	-	-
Tewkesbury	43.0%	43.0%
TOTAL	23.7%	25.0%

Table 12

Alarm System - Tenants' Criticisms

Alarm System	No. of Tenants	Tenants Saying not easy to use	Problems (No. of tenants mentioning)
Bell (push button and pull cord; cord Gent system)	98	7%	Might not reach alarm in emergency (11) Need one in another room (7) Easily mistaken for light switch (5) Cord not near bed (2) Can be set off accidentally (1) Ineffective (1) Should be lower (1) Poorly sited (2) Too low (1) Cord tied up (1)
Bell cord and intercom	64	9%	Might not reach alarm in emergency (2) Unreliable (3) Intercom never explained (2) Intercom inaudible/deaf (2) Needs maintenance (1) Bell push better than cord (1) Longer cord/no tying up (1)

Table 13

Ten Selected Schemes: Expressed Preferences for Laundry Facilities

Scheme	No. Tenants	Tenants Owning Washing Machine	Laundry Room on Scheme	Tenants Owning Spin Drier	Drying Rooms on Scheme	Tenants Laundry Required	Saying Drying Room Required
Bolton	15	73.3%	-	60.0%	-	66.7%	73.3
Bracknell	21	28.6%	Yes	61.9%	-	100.0%	76.2
Caversham	11	9.1%	-	45.5%	-	36.4%	54.5
Cheltenham	18	-	-	44.4%	Yes	72.2%	72.2
Cirencester	15	33.3%	Yes	53.3%	-	93.3%	33.3
Halifax	29	44.8%	-	72.4%	-	48.3%	51.7
Oldham	13	23.1%	-	38.5%	Yes	84.6%	*
Royton	15	40.0%	-	46.7%	-	86.6%	80.0
Surbiton	13	23.1%	-	30.8%	Yes	23.1%	38.5
Tewkesbury	14	21.4%	-	64.3%	Yes	64.3%	60.9
TOTAL	164	31.1%	-	54.3%	-	68.3%	60.9

* No answer

146

Table 14	
Reasons for Non-Usage of Drying Room	
Scheme	Reason
Cheltenham	Too far away (5); Badly equipped (3); Have own drier (3); Not bothered (1); No privacy (1)
Oldham	Have own drier (4); Upstairs (3); Someone else helps (2); Not much use (1); Use launderette, too far away (1); Relations do it (1)
Tewkesbury	Have own drier (6); Not bothered (1); Expensive (1); Someone else helps (1)

Table 15	
Reasons for Non-Usage of Laundry Room	
Scheme	Reason
Bracknell	Do own washing (3); Too far away (2); Too crowded (2); Relatives help (1)
Cirencester	Do own washing (2); Use a laundry (2); Too crowded (1); Too far away (1); Don't have enough washing to fill machine (1); Sometimes use drier only (1)

Table 16a

Schemes with Guest Rooms – Tenants' Attitudes and Levels of Usage

Scheme	No. of Tenants Using Room in Year	No. of Tenants Having Visitors Staying in Flat	No. of Tenants Saying a Guest Room Needed
Bracknell (21 tenants)	4 (19.0%)	6 (29.0%)	19 (95.0%)
Caversham Park (11)	4 (36.0%)	3 (27.0%)	8 (89.0%)
Cheltenham (17)	6 (35.0%)	8 (47.0%)	15 (88.0%)
Cirencester (15)	7 (47.0%)	2 (13.0%)	13 (93.0%)
Halifax (29)	1 (3.0%)	2 (7.0%)	24 (89.0%)
Royton (15)	– –	3 (20.0%)	12 (80.0%)
TOTAL (108 tenants)	22 (20.4%)	24 (22.2%)	91 (84.3%)

Table 16b

Schemes without Guest Rooms - Tenants' Attitudes

Scheme	No. of Tenants Who have Wanted People to Stay		No. of Tenants Having Visitors Staying in Flat		No. of Tenants Saying a Guest Room Needed	
Bolton (15)	1	(7.0%)	1	(7.0%)	5	(33.0%)
Oldham (13)	3	(23.0%)	2	(15.0%)	11	(85.0%)
Surbiton (13)	-		3	(23.0%)	7	(54.0%)
Tewkesbury (14)	4	(29.0%)	6	(43.0%)	7	(50.0%)
TOTAL (55)	8	(14.5%)	12	(21.8%)	30	(54.5%)

*Of the 12 visitors who stayed in tenants flats in the four schemes without a guest room, 11 stayed in the living room on couches, folding beds, etc. and one shared the tenants' bed.

Overall % of tenants saying a guest room needed = 74.2%.

Table 17

Ten Selected Schemes: Social Contact between Tenants

Scheme	Year Opened	No. of Tenants in Scheme	Average of Other Tenants Visited	Average of Tenants Known	Tenants Saying Enough Social Contact
Bolton	1971	37	8.3%	21.4%	60.0%
Bracknell*	1974	52	15.2%	62.1%	95.2%
Caversham	1972	25	4.0%	75.2%	81.8%
Cheltenham*	1968	41	5.9%	70.0%	88.9%
Cirencester	1973	40	5.5%	89.8%	66.7%
Halifax*	1971	72	3.6%	18.6%	100.0%
Oldham	1973	31	10.3%	65.0%	38.5%
Royton	1975	39	4.1%	21.3%	73.3%
Surbiton*	1969	28	15.0%	75.4%	100.0%
Tewkesbury	1972	36	4.7%	60.8%	91.7%

* Schemes with common rooms

150

Table 18a

Social Contact between Tenants on Schemes with Common Room; Attitudes to Common Room Provision

Scheme	Average of Other Tenants Known by Name	Average of Other Tenants Visited	Tenants Saying enough Contact	Tenants Saying Common Room Needed
Bracknell	62.1%	15.2%	95.2%	100.0%
Cheltenham	70.0%	5.9%	88.9%	77.2%
Halifax	18.6%	3.6%	85.1%	100.0%
Surbiton	75.4%	15.0%	100.0%	100.0%
Sub-total	47.0%	8.7%	91.1%	93.8%

Table 18b

Schemes without Common Room Provided: Social Contact and Attitude to Necessity of Common Room

Scheme	Average of Other Tenants Known by Name	Average of Other Tenants Visited	Tenants Saying enough Contact	Tenants Saying Common Room Needed
Bolton	21.4%	8.3%	60.0%	73.3%
Caversham	75.2%	4.0%	81.8%	45.5%
Cirencester	89.8%	5.5%	66.7%	26.7%
Oldham	65.0%	10.3%	38.5%	84.6%
Royton	21.3%	4.1%	73.3%	33.3%
Tewkesbury	60.8%	4.7%	91.7%	53.8%
Sub-total	52.5%	6.1%	67.9%	52.4%
TOTAL	51.0%	7.9%	67.9%	52.4%

Table 18c
Frequency of Use and Activities in Common Room

Scheme	No. of Tenants	Over 1 Per Week	1 per Week Week	1 per Fort- night	Less than 1 per Fortnight	Activities common room used for (% of Tenants)
Bracknell	21	57.1%	-	-	42.9%	Organised events - bingo, films, etc. (86%) Sewing (7%); Occasional event (7%)
Cheltenham	18	-	-	-	100.0%	Occasional event (75%); Read (6%); Needs an organiser (18%)
Halifax	29	27.6%	20.7%	6.9%	44.8%	Organised events - bingo, films, etc. (54%); Play cards (informal) (23%); Club afternoons (19%); Formal meeting (4%)

		Table 19		
		Visiting and Outside Activities		
Scheme	Year	Tenants Previously Living in Area	Average No. of Friends Visited by Tenant each Month	Average No. of Weekly Activities by Tenants
Bolton	1971	80.0%	4.9	0.47
Bracknell*	1974	14.3%	4.3	0.57
Caversham	1972	40.0%	4.8	0.64
Cheltenham*	1968	76.4%	9.2	0.65
Cirencester	1973	33.3%	6.5	0.73
Halifax*	1971	93.1%	3.8	0.59
Oldham	1973	84.6%	3.2	1.00
Royton	1975	33.3%	4.1	0.53
Surbiton*	1969	61.5%	3.5	0.38
Tewkesbury	1972	33.3%	7.6	0.67
TOTAL		57.5%	5.1	0.62

Average for those who lived in area 5.3 friends visited per month
Average for those who did not live in area 4.7 friends visited per month

* Schemes with common rooms

Table 20

Outside Activities Ranked in Order of Frequency

Activity	No. of Tenants	No. of Activities
Church	44	32.6
Over 60's clubs	22	16.3
Social clubs	13	9.6
Voluntary work	9	6.7
Hobby society (needlework, dancing, etc.)	9	6.7
Sport (golf, snooker, races, etc.)	6	4.4
Conservative/Liberal clubs	5	3.7
Church women's societies	4	3.0
Concert	3	2.2
Townswomen's Guild/Women's Institute	3	2.2
Evening classes	2	1.5
Town Council	2	1.5
Freemason	2	1.5
Bingo	2	1.5

Table 21

Ten Selected Schemes: Convenience and Usage of Town Centre

Scheme	Distance to Town Centre (miles)	Tenants Shopping in Town Centre	Average Convenience to Town Centre	Tenants Over Twice Per Week
Bolton	2.0	58.3%	5.0	53.3%
Bracknell	2.0	85.7%	3.1	76.2%
Caversham	1.5	37.5%	4.1	50.0%
Cheltenham	1.5	47.1%	3.4	18.8%
Cirencester	0.33	93.3%	4.4	93.3%
Halifax	0.75	12.0%	4.6	42.9%
Oldham	0.5	70.0%	2.8	50.0%
Royton	0.1	100.0%	5.0	100.0%
Surbiton	0.1	100.0%	5.0	92.3%
Tewkesbury	0.1	100.0%	5.0	92.9%

Table 22

Ten Selected Schemes: Perceived Characteristics of Local Bus Service

Scheme	Distance to Town Centre (miles)	Using Bus to or from Centre	Cost of Bus to Centre	Car Owner-ship	Using Bus 2 per week and over	Convenience for Bus
Bolton	2.0	91.0%	4p	-	60.0%	5.0
Bracknell	2.0	95.0%	15p	4.7%	71.4%	3.0
Caversham	1.5	100.0%	8p	-	60.0%	4.6
Cheltenham	1.5	64.0%	7p	-	35.3%	4.5
Cirencester	0.33	*	3p	13.0%	-	-
Halifax	0.75	60.0%	5p	10.3%	60.7%	4.7
Oldham	0.5	*	4p	15.3%	33.3%	4.1
Royton	0.1	-	4p	-	80.0%	5.0
Surbiton	0.1	22.0%	-	7.6%	38.5%	5.0
Tewkesbury	0.1	-	-	30.0%	-	N/A

* No information

156

Table 23

Ten Selected Schemes: Tenants' Perceptions of Walking Problems in the Area

Scheme	Tenants Saying	Nature of Problem
Bolton	14%	Traffic (2)
Bracknell	57%	No pavements (4) Dangerous steps (2) Traffic (3) Steep slopes (3)
Caversham	-	-
Cheltenham	35	Traffic (6) Poor pavements (1)
Cirencester	86	Poor pavements (14) Traffic (1)
Halifax	32	Steep slopes (9) Traffic (3) Steps (1)
Oldham	77	Subway not liked (5) Steep slopes (4) Traffic (3) Unlit streets (1) Crossing needed (1)
Royton	20	Traffic (3)
Surbiton	15	Steep slope (1) Stiff swing doors (1)
Tewkesbury	15	Poor pavements (1) Need bridge over river (1) Old shops have steps (1)

Table 24

Ten Selected Schemes: Distances and Perceived Convenience to Post Office and Church

Scheme	Distance to Post Office (yards)	Average Convenience Rating	Distance to Church (yards)	Average Convenience Rating
Bolton	440	5.0	100	5.0
Bracknell	1760	1.9	1760	2.1
Caversham	200	4.8	880	4.2
Cheltenham	1240	3.2	100	4.1
Cirencester	835	3.1	750	3.8
Halifax	880	4.2	880	4.2
Oldham	50	4.9	200	4.2
Royton	150	5.0	150	4.7
Surbiton	880	4.2	20	5.0
Tewkesbury	20	5.0	60	5.0

Table 25

Ten Selected Schemes: Number and Types of Facilities said to be Missing

Scheme	Tenants Saying Some Facility Missing	Nature of Facility (Number of Mentions)
Bolton	20.0%	Library (2); Entertainment (1); Cafe (1); Meeting room (1)
Bracknell	95.2%	Post Office (17); Chemist (11); Fresh food shop (7); Other shops (2); Phone box (1); Pub (2); Pillar box (1); Church (1); Outdoor seating (1)
Caversham	18.2%	Cafe (1); Theatre etc. (1)
Cheltenham	44.4%	Fresh food shop (4); Other shops (1); Post Office (2); Chemist (1); Library (4)
Cirencester	20.0%	Telephone (2); Open space (1); Bus stop (1)
Halifax	13.8%	Chemist (2); Pillar box (1); Other shops (1)
Royton	6.7%	Public toilets (1)
Surbiton	30.8%	Theatre etc. (3); Church (1)
Tewkesbury	28.6%	More shops (2); Cheaper shops (1); Access over river (1)

APPENDIX II

HANOVER HOUSING ASSOCIATION AND THE VOLUNTARY HOUSING MOVEMENT

The Hanover and Anchor Housing Associations are the two largest providing sheltered homes for the elderly. Hanover, which was founded in 1963 under the sponsorship of the National Corporation for the Care of Old People, has built more than 125 schemes and is the leading body in the field. Anchor has passed the hundred mark. They are both highly competent organisations building throughout the UK and in many ways typify all that is best in the voluntary housing movement. There are many smaller associations and societies building small schemes of houses, flats and bungalows to meet the local needs of old people.

The voluntary housing movement's origins go back to the nineteenth century almhouse societies and are part and parcel of a tradition of philanthropy and self-help and the widespread efforts to improve housing conditions in the great cities. The Victorian middle class invented the concept of public service and the result has been an impressive number of voluntary bodies and good works of every conceivable kind.

Despite the creation of the Welfare State and a powerful public housing sector, the voluntary movement has enjoyed increasing moral and financial government support and has grown correspondingly. In 1964 the government sponsored National Housing Corporation was set up and was provided with £100 million to lend to appropriate associations established for the express purpose of building non-profit making housing schemes. Since then, the 1974 Housing Act has strengthened the work of the associations by enabling increased amounts of public money to be made available, though there are greater governmental controls on their character and management. During the past two years, more than 1,000 housing associations have been registered under the Act. About 40,000 out of some 275,000 dwellings are built each year by what is sometimes called the 'Third Arm', namely the housing associations. Approximately one quarter of these dwellings are for the aged.

Housing associations registered under the 1974 Act are required to charge 'fair rents' as registered by the Rent Office. It is evident, therefore, that associations are unable to meet capital costs by rental income alone. Finance is made available by either the Housing Corporation or a local authority under mortgage loans repayable over 40 or 60 years. Prospective or existing tenants may often have little or no other source of income than the State pension and there are provisions for the payment of supplementary pensions in such cases. If tenants do not qualify for supplementary pensions it is possible to apply to the local authority for rent allowances. In either case, the sums allowed are assessed by reference to the fair rents fixed.

It is important to appreciate that Hanover's homes are intended for the 'independent' elderly, but with the services of a resident warden. This combination of independence and security encourages elderly people to consider leaving houses which are too large, poorly equipped, unfit, or isolated. Many of those that do make the move would not voluntarily enter a local authority home, however attractive many of them appear to be.

Most of the schemes built by Hanover comprise groups of 24-50 flatlets and/or bungalows, each of which is completely self-contained with its own bedroom, living room, kitchen, bedroom and modern heating system. Only a few have been built with bedsitting room flats and two bedroomed accommodation, and there are flats specifically designed with the needs of disabled people in mind.

MHLG Circular 82/69 lays down definitions of Category I and Category II dwellings. Category I are broadly defined as suitable for the accommodation of "one or two people of the more active kind". These are self-contained units which may be provided with common rooms (lounge, T.V. room, hobbies room). In cases where these do exist, certain other related facilities such as cupboards, storage space and toilet facilities must also be provided. Minimum permissible floor areas are stated and the provision that access from dwellings to the common room need not be covered, although should be as short as possible.

Category II schemes are described as appropriate for the needs of "less active elderly people". In respect of many facilities, fitments and space standards, these two are similar, but in Category II dwellings there must be communal facilities, including a warden's self-contained dwelling, emergency alarm systems connecting each dwelling with the warden's quarters, a common room and laundry room. In these schemes "all accommodation shall be accessible by enclosed and heated circulation areas".

In both category types guest rooms may be provided and in Category II schemes a warden's office may be provided.

There is a resident warden in every scheme (usually this is a man and wife joint post) whose duties are every day administration and attendance to any emergency calls. Each flatlet is linked to the warden's office by an alarm system consisting of several buttons or cords situated in the flat, which, when activated, sound alarms in the warden's accommodation. The warden, though not expected to act as a nurse or home help to tenants, is normally competent to give advice and guidance to tenants about the provision of welfare services.

Hanover's schemes are located whenever possible within a quarter of a mile of shops, a regular bus route, a post office, church and public housing, making important facilities easily accessible to most tenants. The schemes themselves often provide community facilities which may include some or all the following: laundry room, drying room, guest room and communal hall. Dining facilities are provided in only one scheme; some schemes have no community facilities.

APPENDIX III

THE QUESTIONNAIRES

WARDENS' SURVEY

The objective of the warden survey was to identify those aspects of sheltered housing which in the wardens' view were important, or in need of further study. The form of the questionnaire, therefore, was designed to be as wide ranging and open as possible, yet with sufficient structure to enable results to be quantified. A postal questionnaire was used, as all 125 wardens of Hanover schemes in all parts of the country were to be contacted. The questionnaire, therefore, had to be simple to complete.

The questionnaire started with questions to provide basic profile data on the schemes (e.g. number of tenants, type of building, size of warden's flat, etc.). This was followed by a list of 56 specific aspects of the scheme (derived from the literature review) arranged under four headings:

(i)   Internal features (e.g. heating, windows), noise insulation
(ii) External features (e.g. appearance, outdoor seating, parking)
(iii) Location (e.g. with respect to shops, buses, noise sources)
(iv) Management (e.g. warden's duties, contact with head office, contact with other wardens).

In each case the wardens were asked to evaluate the aspect in a simple three point scale (Satisfactory, Indifferent, Unsatisfactory) and to add any comments they might have.

In order to obtain evaluation of features that may have been missed from the list a series of open-ended questions were included at the end of the questionnaire.

TENANTS' SURVEY

The tenants required a more detailed and complex questionnaire to be designed than the wardens' questionnaire. The design was based on the results of the wardens' survey, and upon a small pilot survey which was carried out.

The questionnaire followed the standard practice of having a number of simpler introductory questions, including an open question of likes and dislikes of the scheme, in order to:

(i)   introduce the subject to the respondent, and
(ii) to enable interviewers to establish a rapport with the respondent.

The main body of the questionnaire dealt with the six main issues identified in the wardens survey (heating, safety, noise, privacy, communal facilities and location). In each case the respondents were asked for their:

(i)   Evaluation - using simple dichotomy yes/no responses or scale responses (3-5 point scales). e.g. Are you warm enough at night? How convenient is the scheme to the town centre?
(ii) Behaviour - e.g. How often do you use the common room - what for? How many friends have you on the scheme?
(iii) Attitude - Does this scheme need a common room?

Finally, the respondents were given an opportunity to comment on any other aspects of the schemes they felt were important; and basic profile data was completed (e.g. age, sex, mobility, etc.).

WARDENS QUESTIONNAIRE	Scheme:

1. Number of units in scheme (excluding warden's)?

☐ Bedsitters

☐ Single bedroom units

☐ Double bedroom units

☐ Two bedroom units

2. Number of residents on scheme?

☐ Single (male)

☐ Single (female)

☐ Married

3. How many tenants (if any) are chronically housebound (i.e. 6 months or more)?

☐ Single

☐ Married

4. How many tenants (if any) are wanting to leave the scheme?

5. Has the scheme got any of the following communal facilities? (Please tick the appropriate box)

☐ Guest room

☐ Common room

☐ Laundry

☐ Drying room

☐ Other (specify)_____

6. Is your accommodation in a separate building from the tenants?

| Yes/No | (delete as appropriate)

7. Do you have to use the same entrance to the building as the tenants in order to reach your accommodation?

| Yes/No |

8. How many bedrooms have you got?

9. Have you got an office where you can deal with tenants without interfering with your own home or family?

| Yes/No |

10. Do you have a deputy warden or an assistant for the periods when you are off-duty or away from the scheme?

| Yes/No |

11. Is your scheme satisfactory in the following respects?
The following table is a list of different aspects of Hanover Schemes. Against each aspect there is a scale with three values: 1 - Unsatisfactory; 2 - Indifferent; 3 - Satisfactory. For each aspect, please tick the one which, in your opinion, applies to your scheme. If something does not apply to your scheme, or you have some particular comments to make, please use the space provided.

ASPECT	Unsatisfactory	Indifferent	Satisfactory	SPECIAL COMMENTS
Internal Features				
Tenants Heating (specify type)				
(a)	1	2	3	
(b)	1	2	3	
(c)	1	2	3	
Cost of heating to tenants	1	2	3	
Ventilation	1	2	3	
Windows	1	2	3	
Storage facilities to tenants	1	2	3	

165

ASPECT	Unsatisfactory	Indifferent	Satisfactory	SPECIAL COMMENTS
Size of tenants dwellings	1	2	3	
Noise insulation, from neighbours, through wall, ceiling, etc.	1	2	3	
Noise insulation from outside (traffic, playgrounds, etc.)	1	2	3	
Safety				
Alarm call system - state type				
....	1	2	3	
Fire safety	1	2	3	
Other safety features (non-slip surfaces, handrails, pass-key system, etc.)	1	2	3	
Other internal features				
Warden's dwelling	1	2	3	
Warden's privacy	1	2	3	
Storage of warden's work equipment	1	2	3	
Communal facilities	1	2	3	
Site features				
Type of dwellings (use scale(s) which apply to your scheme:				
(a) Bungalow	1	2	3	
(b) 1 storey	1	2	3	
(c) 2-3 storey	1	2	3	
(d) Over 4 storey	1	2	3	
Privacy of tenants from each other	1	2	3	
Privacy of scheme from surrounding areas	1	2	3	
Security of the scheme	1	2	3	
Layout of the site	1	2	3	
Landscaping of the site	1	2	3	
Appearance of the buildings	1	2	3	
Gardening opportunities for tenants (are they provided?) (Yes/No)	1	2	3	

ASPECT	Unsatisfactory	Indifferent	Satisfactory	SPECIAL COMMENTS
Management				
Warden's duties:				
(a) Cleaning	1	2	3	
(b) Contact with tenants	1	2	3	
(c) Repairs, etc.	1	2	3	
(d) Other duties (specify)				
....	1	2	3	
Arrangements for off-duty	1	2	3	
Contact with other wardens (Do you have any? Yes/No)	1	2	3	
Contact with Hanover	1	2	3	
Number of tenants on scheme	1	2	3	
Suitability of tenants for scheme	1	2	3	

12. Have you any comments on particularly good features of your scheme?

13. What feature(s) of the scheme, in your opinion, could be most improved upon?

14. What features, in your opinion, could be left out in new schemes (if anything)?

15. What additional features, if any, would you like to see in new schemes?

16. Have you any other comments on particular problems which have arisen in your schemes?

167

ASPECT	Unsatisfactory	Indifferent	Satisfactory	SPECIAL COMMENTS
Clothes drying area	1	2	3	
Car parking	1	2	3	
Paths on site (safety etc)	1	2	3	
Lighting on site	1	2	3	
Outdoor seating	1	2	3	
Refuse collection arrangement	1	2	3	
Location				
Traffic hazards	1	2	3	
Noise levels	1	2	3	
Slope of site location	1	2	3	
Air quality	1	2	3	
Other environmental factors (wind, looks of surroundings, etc.)	1	2	3	
Bus service (cost, frequency, etc.)	1	2	3	
Convenience of Location				**Estimated Distance**
As well as giving each aspect a score, please estimate the distance to the facility mentioned				Tick which scale you are using: miles yards kilometres metres
Town centre	1	2	3	
General grocery store	1	2	3	
Chemist	1	2	3	
Post Office	1	2	3	
Church	1	2	3	
Doctor	1	2	3	
How would you rate the general accessibility of your scheme?	1	2	3	

TENANTS QUESTIONNAIRE	Interview Number ☐

Introduction

I am doing a survey for Aston University on behalf of the Hanover Housing Association into what tenants think about their flats. I will eventually be interviewing half of the tenants on this particular scheme. Would you mind answering some questions about your dwelling and the scheme? (Assure the respondent, if necessary, that their replies will be treated confidentially, and will not be passed on to anyone. Point out that you are not asking for their names.)

A. (General Questions)
1. How long have your lived in this flat? (Code years, months)
2. How satisfied are you with it? (Use card 1 as a prompt)
3. What things do you like about your flat and the scheme? (Write in)

4. What things do you dislike about your flat and the scheme ? (Write in)

B. (Now there are some questions about the heating in your flat)
5. How satisfied are you with the heating? (Use card 1 as a prompt. Explain, if necessary, "taking the cost, effectiveness and ease of operating heating into account.")
6. Is your dwelling warm enough in very cold weather:
   (a) at night (Code 0-No; 1-Yes)
   (b) during the day (Code 0-No; 1-Yes)
7. (Make a note of the main heating system; ask if necessary)
   ....
   Do you usually use the main heating system (specify "in winter" if necessary. Code 0-No;1-Yes). If not, why not:

8. Do you use any additional or alternative form of heating? (Code 0-No; Code 1-Yes). If yes: what type? .... why?

169

9. In what way do you usually pay for the heating? (e.g. in rent, coin box, etc.)

☐

10. How much did your last heating bill come to? (If known):
Amount (£)
Period (tick) week; month; quarter; ....
Notes (e.g. includes lighting, cooking, etc.)

☐☐☐☐
☐☐

11. Heating is expensive for everyone nowadays, but do you think that your main form of heating is more expensive than normal? (Code 0-No; 1-Yes)

☐

12. Have you any other comments about the heating of your flat?

☐☐
☐☐

C. (Now I want to turn to some other aspects of your flat)

13. Are you bothered at all about noise in your flat (Code 0-No; 1-Yes). If yes:
    (a) How noisy is it (Use prompt card 2)
    (b) Where does the noise come from mainly?

☐
☐
☐☐

    (c) What type of noise is it? (e.g. continuous, intermittent, high pitched, etc.)

☐☐

    (d) What time of day is it worst?

☐

14. Can you usually hear your neighbour's T.V., radio, or conversation? (Code 0-No; 1-Yes)

☐

D. (Safety: Note what type of alarm call system is installed, ask if necessary) ....

☐

15. Do you think that the alarm call system is necessary in a scheme like this? (Code 0-No; 1-Yes)

☐

16. Have you ever used the alarm call ? (Code 0-No; 1-Yes). If yes:
How often (in last 12 months)?
Was it effective? (Code 0-No; 1-Yes)

☐
☐☐
☐

17. Is your system easy to use, if you should need it? (Code 0-No; 1-Yes) If no
What is wrong with it?

☐
☐☐

170

18. How well, in your opinion, is your dwelling designed to help prevent minor accidents? (Use prompt card 3; explain, if necessary, "e.g. no steps, grab-bars, in bathroom, cupboards at an easy height").

19. Are there any changes or additions you would make in order to improve safety generally? (Prompt, e.g. from minor accidents, fire, or in the case of sudden illness)

20. Are there too many safety features? (Code 0-No; 1-Yes).

E. (Now I would like to turn to communal facilities)
(Note if the tenants has the following - ask if necessary)
T.V.   Code 0-No; 1-Yes
Washing machine   Code 0-No; 1-Yes
Drier   Code 0-No; 1-Yes

21. If the scheme has a laundry room:
    (a) How often, if at all, do you use the laundry room? (Code: 1- over 1 per week; 2- 1 per week; 3- 1 per fortnight, 4- less than 1 per fortnight)
    (b) If not used at all: why not:

22. If the scheme has a drying room:
    (a) How often, if at all, do you use the drying room? (Code as for 21)
    (b) If not used at all, why not?

23. All schemes: How do you normally do your washing? (Or does someone do it for you? Do you use a laundry service, etc.?)

24. All schemes: Do you personally think that this scheme needs a laundry room with a washing machine? (Code 0-no; 1-Yes)

25. All schemes: Do you personally think that this scheme needs a drying room? (Code 0-No; 1-Yes)

26. If the scheme has a common room:
    (a) How often, if at all, do you use the common room? (Code as for 21)
    (b) What activities do you join in in the common room?

171

27. All schemes: How many tenants do you know by name (surname)?

28. All schemes: How many tenants have you visited, or have visited you in the last week?

29. All schemes: Is there enough social contact between you and the other tenants? (Code 0-No; 1-Yes)

30. All schemes: Did you live in this town/area before moving into this scheme (Code 0-No; 1-Yes)

31. All schemes: How many friends and relatives in this town/area have you visited in the last month, or have visited you?

32. All schemes: How often, if at all, do you go to activities outside the scheme? (Prompt: church, OAP club, specialist societies, etc.)
    Activity (list)   Frequency
    1.
    2.
    3.
    4.

33. All schemes: Do you think that this scheme needs a common room? (Code 0-No; 1-Yes) If yes (and no common room on scheme) what for?

34. If scheme has a guest room: How often, if at all, have you made use of the guest room in the last year?
    If not used: Have you had anyone stay in your own flat in the last year? (Code 0-No; 1-Yes)

35. If scheme is without guest room: Have you had anyone to stay in the last year? (Code 0-No; 1-Yes)
    If yes: Where did they stay?

    If no: Have you wanted to have anyone to stay? (Code 0-No; 1-Yes)

36. All schemes: Do you think that this scheme needs a guest room (i.e. a communal spare bedroom)? (Code 0-No; 1-Yes)

37. If scheme has a hobbies room: How often if at all, do you use the hobbies room?
    ....

F. (Now I would like to ask some questions about the location of this scheme)

38. Do you think that this scheme is:
    (1) Too separated; (2) About right; (3) Not separated enough, from other housing in the area?

172

39. Do children use the grounds for playing? (Code 0-no; 1-Yes) If yes: Does this bother you personally? (Code 0-no; 1-Yes)	▯
40. Do people use the grounds as a short-cut? (Code 0-No; 1-Yes) If yes: Does this bother you personally? (Code 0-No; 1-Yes)	▯
41. Are there any changes or improvements you would make in the scheme to make it more or less private? (Code 0 - no change; 1 - more private; 2 - less private; write in comments)	▯
42. How convenient is the scheme for shopping? (Use prompt card 4, add "shopping in general, e.g. groceries", if necessary)	▯
43. How often do you do any shopping? (Code 1 - every day; 2 - 2-4 times per week; 3 - 1 per week; 4 - less than 1 per week; 5 - mobile shop used; 6 - shopping done by someone; 7 -other (specify)	▯
44. Where do you do your shopping?	▯
If not town centre: (a) How convenient is your scheme to the town centre? (Use prompt card 4)	▯
(b) How often do you go to the town centre? (Code as for 43)	▯
(c) How do you get there?	▯
45. How convenient is your scheme to a post office? (Use card 4)	▯
46. How convenient is your scheme to a church? (use card 4)	▯
47. Have you got a car (in the household)? (Code-0-No; 1-Yes)	▯
48. How convenient is the bus service into town (if applicable)? (Use card 4). (Note how much it costs (single) to the town centre, and whether this is an OAP concessionary fare)	▯
49. How often do you usually use the bus? (Code as for 43)	▯
50. Would you like to be nearer the town centre? (Code 0-no; 1-Yes)	▯
51. Are there any particular problems with walking (or travelling if disabled) in this area? (Prompt: "e.g. steep slopes, steps, heavy traffic". (Code -0 - No; 1-Yes) If yes: what are they?	▯

52. Are there any necessary facilities which are missing in this area (i.e. in the neighbourhood of the scheme)? (Code 0-No; 1-Yes)
If yes: What are they?

G. Finally, have you any other comments about your flat, the scheme, or its location; anything which has not been mentioned so far?

Interviewers: Please note whether respondent is:

    0 - Male; 1 - Female
    0 - Ambulant; 1 - Non-ambulant
    0 - Single/Widowed; 1 - Married
    Age (if possible)

    Type of unit:

    0 - Bedsitter
    1 - Single bedroomed
    2 - Double bedroomed

174

APPENDIX IV

HANOVER HOUSING ASSOCIATION - TERMS OF REFERENCE

PROPOSED FEASIBILITY STUDY OF HOUSING DESIGN FOR THE ELDERLY

"The Association is anxious to incorporate and try out, in its housing schemes for the elderly, whatever experimental features seem likely to have promise. Only in so doing, it believes, will it keep abreast both of current needs of the elderly and modern technical developments, marrying the two where possible and appropriate. Features to be tried may vary from the small, such as door handles or tap handles; to the larger such as methods of heating or insulation or the design of windows or baths; to the overall concept of an old person's dwelling and its relationship to family housing and social amenities. Yet the Association does not wish, indeed cannot afford, to waste money in inconclusive experiments. It therefore was decided, with the support of the National Corporation for the Care of Old People, first to promote a feasibility study, on which it is hoped a policy of sound experimental work can be based, and for which funds can be sought.

The Association is therefore wishing to commission a person or persons suitably qualified to carry out a study with the following objectives:

(a) To put together from existing sources, whatever information there is on experiments relevant to special housing for the elderly.

(b) To obtain ideas on other work that could usefully be done.

(c) To provide some assessment of the feasibility of the Association carrying out such work and being able to draw varied conclusions in due course, for its own benefit and that of housing policies generally, about the value of the experimental features or design concerned.

(d) To indicate the expenditure likely to be involved in

175

such work, the extent to which existing sources of funds may be drawn on to meet it, and the resultant net cost to the Association of undertaking it.

The Association anticipates that this study will take 6-12 months, and would like to discuss terms for the carrying out of the study with individuals or institutions that might be able to do it. They are asked to get in touch with the Association through the undersigned ...."

HANOVER HOUSING ASSOCIATION - ADDITIONAL NOTE

Proposed feasibility study of housing design for the elderly by the Department of Architectural, Planning and Urban Studies of the University of Aston

1. Sound insulation: how far tenants are troubled by road noise, railway, other tenants' wireless/TV, other tenants' plumbing, and how far these matters can be overcome by better check list or different design.

2. Refuse disposal for flats. What methods are satisfactory and what not. Can new ways be tried?

3. Common parts - inside and outside buildings; are stairways, gardens, open ground, car parks, abused by the public, children, vandals? If so, how can this be obviated by better design, or by such technical devices as electronic porters for outer doors to buildings, movable posts in car park areas, etc.?

4. Telephones; does present use of private or public 'phones indicate what is ideally needed and how HHA could help provide more useful means of communication, e.g. by shared facilities?

Other design features which need examination, but which may not be within Aston's metier are:-

5. Flooring - what ought HHA to be providing?

6. Kitchen layout and design, e.g. room for table, better window control.

176

7. Ditto for bathrooms, and should some availability of showers be tried?

8. Lifts.

9. Positioning of doors e.g. kitchen doors opening inwards against cupboards, etc.

10. Window sills - difficulties caused by depth.

11. Built-in wardrobes - are these necessary, or do tenants prefer to provide their own?

12. Bedrooms - where there are two, is the second one large enough?

13. Bedsit flats - do the tenants like these where they are provided? At the present time, Hanover is against provision of bed-sitters, but these have been provided in some of our London schemes and appear to be popular, particularly since the rent is lower than the normal one bedroom flat.

14. Provision and use of common rooms/laundry/guest rooms. Tenants reaction to these would be interesting.

15. Glass panels in front doors or over to light passages inside flats.

PART II

Appendix I: Literature Review

Appendix II: Selective Bibliography

INTRODUCTION

The desk study forms part of a research project begun in January 1976, to be completed at the end of the year, commissioned by Hanover Housing Assocation.

The work involved a survey of the attitudes of wardens on all sheltered housing schemes built by Hanover and the use of this information as a guide for the content of a survey of the tenants of selected schemes. An interim report was presented to Hanover for discussion by the Housing Management Sub-Committee in April 1976, at which time the wardens' survey had been completed and the tenant survey was being organised.

Although forming part of the final report the desk study can be treated as a free-standing unit to be read without reference to the empirical work carried out for Hanover, and this is how it is presented here. In the final report the discussion of the research carried out at the selected schemes further amplifies the comments made in the desk study and relates them to the contribution that Hanover is making in this area, comparing and contrasting the reviewed area with this study and present conclusions and recommendations arising from the results.

LITERATURE REVIEW

This literature review concentrates upon sheltered housing and the associated design etc. issues. A large amount of work primarily relating to the disabled and the elderly generally and the provision of services for the elderly has thus not directly been referred to. The review has not only been based upon published literature, but also upon discussions with those currently undertaking research and with officers of Hanover themselves. It is necessary first to outline what is understood by the term 'sheltered housing' for the elderly. Sheltered housing is generally held to include bungalows, houses, flats or flatlets which are under the overall responsibility of a warden.(1) Although according to this definition there is no need for the dwellings to be grouped, in view of the requirement of warden supervision the dwellings usually are grouped.

The concept of sheltered housing, as opposed to residential homes where the element of supervision and care is greater, has only arisen in the past 25 years. The Ministry of Housing and Local Government recommended the idea of sheltered housing to local authorities in 1957 (2), and in the next five years provided design and layout guides.(3) The bulk of the original research related to sheltered housing has been carried out within the MHLG and also the Department of the Environment, and this review rests heavily on that work. The principles of sheltered housing as they evolved from the Ministry work were enshrined in the Ministry Circular 82/69 'Housing Standards and Costs, Accommodation Specially Designed for Old People'.(4)

The involvement of housing associations in the provision of sheltered housing began in 1957 when local authorities were given permissive powers to assist housing associations by loans, welfare grants to wardens, etc. Various circulars encouraged local authorities to use these powers (5) and further aid appeared in 1964 with the setting up of the Housing Corporation with access to funds for housing societies and associations to build.(6) To date the main piece of research work carried out into sheltered housing built by a housing association is that commissioned by Hanover and carried out by CURS, University of Birmingham. (7) This research has also been drawn upon in this review.

In order to introduce some organisation into the presentation of this literature review two rules have been followed so that the information organised is,

(i)   in a form which would be comparable with the Hanover Design Brief.(8)
(ii) in a readily usable format for the design and evaluation of the surveys.

182

As a result the information was divided into four useful categories which were retained in the wardens' survey:-

(i)   Internal design
(ii)   External design and layout
(iii)   Location of scheme
(iv)   Management of scheme.

Within these categories the information was sub-divided into issues which appeared to be self-contained, and which correspond generally to items in Hanover's design requirements.

The review itself forms Appendix I of the final report and is complemented by a selected bibliography of literature and research in Appendix II. It should be noted that a small number of bibliographies and directories already exist (9) (and one has now been issued by the National Building Agency) and it was not felt to be necessary to duplicate all but the most relevant references.

NOTES

1.   G. Sumner and R. Smith, 'Planning Local Authority Services for the Elderly', London, George Allen and Unwin, 1960
2.   MHLG Circular 55/57, 'Housing for Old People'
3.   MHLG, 'Flatlets for Old People', HMSO, 1958
       MHLG, 'More Flatlets for Old People', HMSO, 1960
       MHLG, 'Design Bulletin 1, Some Aspects of Designing for Old People', HMSO, 1962
       MHLG, 'Design Bulletin 2, Grouped Flatlets for Old People', HMSO, 1962
4.   MHLG Circular 82/69, 'Housing Standards and Costs, Accommodation Specially Designed for Old People'
5.   MHLG Circular 12/62, 'Housing Associations in England and Wales'
       MHLG Circular 41/64
6.   G. Sumner and R. Smith, op. cit.
7.   D. Mercer and T. Muir, 'Hanover Housing Assocation Assessment Study', CURS, University of Birmingham, 1969
8.   Hanover Housing Association, 'Architectural Design Requirements', HHA 152/D7
9.   See, for example:
       G. Sumner and R.Smith, op. cit.
       US Department of Housing and Urban Development, 'The Built Environment for the Elderly and the Handicapped -A Bibliography'

Numbered references in text refer to Bibliography in Appendix II; ADR numbers relate to Hanover Architectural Design Requirements HHA152/D7.

INTERNAL ASPECTS

Type of Building (ADR 3.1)

Research findings on the most desirable type of buildings for sheltered housing have revolved around two main issues; the relative acceptability of bungalows versus flatted dwellings; and the optimum (or more often the maximum) number of storeys for flatted developments. The alternative of conversions of existing buildings has scarcely been re-reviewed since the shift towards new building in the 50's. (10, 101)

Early practice, and some research, pointed to a slight preference towards bungalows and ground floor dwellings, particularly by the not so active elderly. (35, 73, 79) More recent research, which has included surveys of a wider range of housing than the previous work, has shown that, provided the lifts are adequate, higher storeys are accepted by the majority (32, 53) and indeed preferred by some. (57) The increased feeling of privacy and security on the upper floors has been noted as an important consideration. (10, 79)

Given the flexibility of residential preferences, it would appear that considerations such as site characteristics, density requirements and economic viability would be paramount in choice of building type.

Type of unit (ADR 3.2)

The accepted type of dwelling unit for sheltered housing has also demonstrated a development over the last twenty years.

In the first Ministry Guidelines, bedsitting rooms with shared toilet and bathroom facilities were recommended. (76) The acceptable number of tenants sharing facilities fell in the 60's, and at the same time there was an increasing demand for a separate bedroom. (27, 39, 56, 79)

Although the majority of the elderly would prefer the greater separation of eating and sleeping functions implied by a separate bedroom, one piece of research has suggested that fears of the extra costs (rent) involved means that many tenants retain a preference for a bed-sitter. Indeed, the previous study of Hanover schemes found that 33 per cent of those residents who had separate bedrooms would prefer a bedsitter if this meant lower rent. (73)

The demands expressed reflect not only a general rise in expectations and standards, but also relate to the recognition that the needs of elderly households do not always differ markedly from other small households. Thus, for married elderly couples there is a demand for a second bedroom in some cases (e.g. for visitors or to enable the couple to sleep separately in case of illness, etc.). (73)

Hanover requirements suggest that the majority of flats should be one-bedroomed, two-person flats with up to a sixth of the units being two-bedroomed, three-person flats. However, this mix does not appear to give the maximum amount of choice of unit type, particularly given the fact that the majority of sheltered housing tenants are single (women). (7) The provision of a range of units from bed-sitters to two-bedroomed units would give greater flexibility. (43) However, it should be noted that Hanover provide two-person units which are suitable for either one or two persons.

Size of unit (ADR 5.2.1; 5.3.1; 5.4.1)

The size of units, and the rooms contained in them, has been based since 1969 on the minimum standards set out in MHLG Circular 82/69. The circular stipulates a minimum area, including storage space, of $32.6m^2$ for a single person flat and $47.5m^2$ for a two person flat. Within this overall standard the suggested minimum size of a double bedroom is $11.5m^2$ and of a bedsitter $13m^2$. The minimum size for a single bedroom laid down in the previous Housing Manual (57) was 6.5-7.5m^2.

Evidence from the research suggests that bedrooms which are close to the minimum size are not felt to be satisfactory by most residents. (31, 35, 57, 79) Bedsitters under 15m^2 and single bedrooms smaller than 8.6m^2 have been found to cause some dissatisfaction. (31, 57) The size of bedsitting rooms has also been found to have a marked effect on overall satisfaction. (57) The size of living rooms appears to produce little comment from tenants.

Hanover size guidelines of 6.5m^2 for a single bedroom thus appear to be too small, whereas the double bedroom size of 12.5m^2 is probably sufficient. 65m^2 refers only to second bedrooms, not to the case where only one bedroom exists.

However, several pieces of research have noted that the design of the rooms as well as the size is critical, particularly as the elderly are often in possession of large and bulky furniture (7, 73) and have been found, naturally, not always, to follow the architect's ideas of where the furniture should be placed in a room. (43, 79)

In this latter respect kitchen size is less of a problem as a large proportion of fitted storage space is usually provided, although as refrigerators and washing machines become more widespread, space has to be included for them. (35, 73) Once again, a general desire for more than the current minimum (e.g. Hanover requirement 6.5m^2) has been found (10, 53) and with a layout which enables meals to be taken in the kitchen if required.

Layout

Three issues related to layout are raised in the reviewed research. The first issue applies specifically to those schemes in which washing and toilet facilities are shared. As this does not apply to Hanover schemes in general, this issue will not be dealt with here (see 27, 31, 56, 79) for discussion of this).

The second issue, or rather set of issues, is the particular layout problems within the dwellings which have been found to occur on some schemes. For example, having the toilet only reachable through the bathroom and through the bedrooms, thus forming a potential danger spot; (6) the undesirability of having a bathroom opening directly into a living room; (4) the problems of having only one 'designed' position for the bed in a bed-sitting room; (6) the preference for a separate kitchen rather than just a cooking alcove. (57, 79) Some further points under this issue will be raised again under 'Safety'. These detailed aspects of design are also the subject of research currently in progress at the Welsh School of Architecture. (103)

The third issue relating to layout is the possible effect the layout of the scheme as a whole (e.g. position of dwelling entrances, location of communal areas, etc.) has upon the social relationships in the scheme. This is an extremely difficult topic to discuss, not least because of the number of variables involved (see for example Michelson, (74)) for a general discussion. All other things being equal, and this implies, for example, social compatability among residents, the layout and design can have an effect on social behaviour either by facilitating or hindering contacts. There is a danger in thinking in deterministic terms and in assuming that 'the elderly' form a cohesive social group with common values and aspirations (e.g. the assumption that where there are no visual barriers and separate entrance doors, the occupants are more likely to talk to other tenants (58) may not hold true if the contact breeds hostility rather than friendliness).

It is easier to consider the effects of layout in a negative sense, i.e. what behaviour is constrained. The division of a scheme into separate blocks means that friendships between blocks are less likely to be formed. (53) The question of the provision (or not) of common rooms will be discussed later.

Storage (ADR 5.1.5; 5.1.6; 5.4.2)

As with the dwelling unit there are two main issues relating to storage; size, and design and convenience. (73) Size requirements are set out in the MHLG Circular 82/69 and are $2.6m^2$ for single person flats, $3m^2$ for two person flats (slightly more in bungalows). Hanover design requirements are for a large store (rather than two small ones) which can accommodate a wheelchair; and for a linen store with a minimum of two shelves.

The main storage features which have occurred as problems in the research are:

(i)   Insufficient shelving (73, 79)

(ii) The need to specify a maximum shelf height. The generally accepted maximum is 1.5m (Hanover requirements - no shelves in kitchen over 1.52m) and it has also been suggested that the space between the highest shelf and the ceiling should be boarded up 'to prevent temptation'. (5, 6, 34, 79)

(iii) The need to specify a minimum shelf height has also been mentioned, to avoid the need for tenants to bend down. One suggested minimum is 0.6m from the floor, although it is recognised that having this limit makes it difficult to comply with the storage space requirements. (6) Circular 92/69 sets down a minimum height of 0.3m for linen cupboard shelves.

(iv) The problem of the tenants having to use their own furniture which is often bulky and unsuited to the flat design. The provision of fitted clothing storage space removes the need for the elderly to bring their own furniture (however, it should be noted that some tenants may want to retain their furniture). (79)

Bathroom (ADR 5.5)

Much of the discussion relating to bathroom provision in the research has been concentrated upon shared facilities, and the optimum number of households to each bathroom. (31, 79) As this issue hardly arises on Hanover schemes it is not discussed here.

Two other issues occur in the research: safety aspects of the bathroom, and the choice of installation, particularly the choice between baths and showers.

189

The difficulty with providing safety features which are designed for the most vulnerable tenants is that they may be misused or resented by the majority, and possibly therefore be of no use in an emergency. (56) However, there is some evidence that most safety features are used and appreciated by most tenants, even the healthy ones. For example, in one study three quarters of the tenants were found to use the hand grips on the bath. (56) The features which were most often provided are non-skid bath surfaces, low bath and lift bars, outward opening door with lock operable from the outside. (4, 68) One feature which is a source of annoyance to many tenants is the low and small bath often provided; an ordinary bath would be preferred. (56, 73)

The question of the relative desirability of showers versus baths which is unresolved in the research, a reflection of the varying personal preferences. Unfamiliarity with showers in the past has perhaps made them less popular (56), but in one study 25 per cent of the tenants would prefer showers to baths. (90) One suggestion made, usually for those schemes which have communal bathrooms, is to provide at least one communal shower for the use of those who want it, or who are unable to take a bath.

The control of water temperature is critical and contributed to the fears of tenants in one study. (10) A pre-set control may be necessary as a safety device to prevent the accidental selection of very hot water. (68)

Windows   (ADR 5.1.8; 5.1.9; 5.2.2; 5.3.2; 5.4.3; 5.5.3)

This section deals with window design rather than the outlook from windows which will be discussed later. In the previous Hanover study window design was found to be one of the most criticised features of internal design. (73) From this study and others it is possible to outline six design points which require consideration:

(i)   Windows should be easy to operate. Problems usually arise not so much from poor design as from poor construction leading to windows which can only be opened or closed with difficulty. (53)

(ii)   Windows should be easy to clean, preferably with the ability to clean the outside of the window from the flat. Many tenants wish to clean their own windows rather than to have it done. (34, 53)

(iii) Ventilation is best provided by small controllable openings (including louvres) rather than large opening windows alone which are usually disliked. (34, 73)

(iv)   Large windows, including bay windows, are generally not liked for a variety of reasons: e.g. heat loss, difficulties of cleaning and cost of curtaining. (34, 73)

(v)   Low sills are preferred. In one study looking out of the window provided satisfaction for half the tenants interviewed. (53) It should be noted, however, that this applies more to the living room than to the bedrooms; and for less active tenants. (73)

(vi)   The depth of sill should be such that tenants can reach windows for opening or cleaning. This applies particularly in kitchens where the sink is positioned in front of the window. (79)

The conclusion reached in the Hanover study, in which the detailed window design features of sixteen different schemes were compared, was that the most favoured window design was the side hung casement window with a small transom window over a fixed panel. (73) In schemes with this type of window complaints were restricted to the position of windows and difficulties of opening rather than design.

Hanover design requirements incorporate most of these points except recommendations on size of windows and ease of cleaning from inside.

Ventilation   (ADR 5.1.8)

The problems of ventilation have not received any particular attention in the reviewed research. Problems that have been noted are often related partly to window design, e.g. the existence of draughts (73), and the necessity to open main windows to obtain any ventilation. (35, 73) In the United States full air conditioning in most climates is recommended (68), but this has yet to be applied in the UK. Two aspects are important:

(i)   Ventilation to prevent the problem of condensation, particularly in the kitchen and bathroom.

(ii) Ability to have ventilation during the night without having (unlocked) open main windows.

Doors   (ADR 5.1.10; 5.5.1; 5.6.1)

Doors, being a relatively straightforward feature, have received little attention beyond ensuring that they should be suitable for wheelchair users, and be operated by those elderly who have arthritic hands. Detailed door design for the disabled is covered adequately elsewhere. (44)

Heating   (ADR 6.1; 6.2; 6.3; 6.4; 6.5; 6.6)

The provision of heating in sheltered housing has changed radically over the last 20 years. It was at first assumed for example that the elderly would prefer traditional methods of heating, despite the considerable work involved in operating traditional coal fires. Early research found coal fires were satisfactory for over half the interviewed tenants, but the necessity for additional heating in cold periods and keeping the fires clean were major problems. (56, 90) Non-burning heating systems have been almost exclusively recommended over the last decade (68, 79), and have been well accepted by the elderly. The issues which have arisen in the last decade with respect to heating systems are the adequacy of heating, the ease of control of the heating, and the cost of heating.

Adequacy of heating   MHLG Circular 82/69 recommended a minimum standard of heating of 21°c in main living areas in flats and 15.6^{o}c in circulation areas of grouped schemes when the external temperature is -1°c. The Hanover study identified two problems which result in these conditions not being met (73):

(i)   When not all areas of a flat are heated by the main system; this often applies to block storage and warm air systems. The absence of heating in all rooms necessitates the use of auxiliary heating which is often costly.

(ii) When the system is not effective enough. This applies particularly to storage systems (block or

192

underfloor storage heating) when the rate of heat supply tails off in the afternoon and early evening. (73)

Ease of control Individual heat control is recommended for sheltered housing (68) and difficulties only appear to arise when control is difficult (e.g. the inflexibility of storage systems) or when tenants' misunderstanding of the mode of operation leads to the mis-use of the heating. (45, 53) The most usual forms of mis-use are the attempted economies by turning heating on and off. However, in comparison with traditional coal fires the maintenance and control requirements of current systems are negligible.

Cost of heating This aspect, along with the question of adequacy, appears to be the most critical one with regard to heating. (10) Several studies have shown that space heating systems are simply not used if the costs are high, with obvious detrimental effects on the health of the tenants. (35, 57, 73) There are two main aspects to this question:

(i) Actual cost of heating: the necessity of installing low capital cost heating systems in order to keep within the housing cost yardstick, has often resulted in the use of systems with high running costs. (6) The actual cost is critical to the elderly who have low disposable incomes. (92)

(ii) Perceived or effective cost of heating. This depends on the system of charging for heating costs. The disadvantages of having separate quarterly bills for gas and electricity has been realised both in relation to sheltered housing, and for the elderly generally. (7, 92) Most gas and electricity boards now operate installment payment schemes. In some sheltered housing schemes standard heating charges are made throughout the year (often included in the rent) with rebates given at the end of the year if less heating is used. This charging method is popular. (5, 53) In the cases where individual use of heating is not monitored complaints are made that it is impossible for the individual to make any savings if they wish.

Summarising these points and relating them to the different heating systems available is not easy as a full comparison is not available. The previous Hanover study is the most useful work in which gas-fired radiators followed by underfloor heating, came out best. (73) Warm air systems were not liked (ineffective, noisy, etc.) although they have been recommmended in other schemes. (4) Ceiling heating, which is recommended in the Hanover Design Requirements has not been covered in any of the surveys and there is no evidence yet as to its acceptability. It is now understood that Hanover has recently altered its policy on ceiling heating and no longer includes this in its design requirements.

Safety features   (ADR 5.5.2; 5.6.4; 5.6.5; 6.8; 6.15)

A well established list of safety features in sheltered housing has evolved over the last 20 years - including hand-rail provision, non-slip floor surfacing, no thresholds on doors, avoidance of isolated steps, safety shut-offs on gas appliances, lights accessible for bulb changing, shallow stair treads and so on. (35, 68)

Such features should be available, but not obtrusive. (43) Most of these features, plus those relating to bathrooms and kitchens which have already been covered, are incorporated into the Hanover Design Requirements.   Bathroom and toileting aids are the subject of current research at the University of Leeds. (19)

There are two associated problems with the provision of safety features:

(i)   Non-use or mis-use, resulting usually from poor location of safety features, e.g. grab-bars, bath poles in inconvenient positions. (5)

(ii)   Misunderstanding or ignorance of a safety feature which leads to mis-use or negation of its effect. Notable examples are non-slip surfaces being covered by rugs (56), and bolts and chains on tenants' front doors nullifying the effect of wardens having a pass-key. (73)

194

Alarm call system   (ADR 6.16; 6.17)

The need for some emergency alarm system in sheltered housing has been recognised from the start of sheltered housing (31), and is reflected in MHLG Circular 82/69. Although such a system, like the other safety features, may be an unpleasant reminder of ageing to the tenant (10), the need for it is generally accepted by the elderly themselves.

The requirements and effectiveness of alarm systems on the market have been extensively researched by the Institute of Consumer Ergonomics. (36, 37) Their full report, including laboratory tests of systems available up to early 1974, is the major work in this area from which the following points can be drawn as a summary:

(i)   The alarm activation points must be within easy reach of the users. (10, 36, 73) As most people remain immobile after the incident, this requirement suggests an activator which has to be carried continuously. (36) However, this is not always practical, and with a lower risk group as in sheltered housing (Category 1) may not be necessary.

(ii)   Activation must be easy. (36) An associated problem is that of accidental operation, particularly before tenants become familiar with the system or by visitors. (73) Activation points should therefore be distinct.

(iii) The system must be effective, i.e. the warden's (or deputy's) attention should always be gained, and the location of the call identified. The problem of misuse or of hoax calls is reduced if the caller can be identified, i.e. without the tenant being able to cancel the signal. (73)

(iv)   The system must be reliable. In terms of the choice of the system the after sales checks and services are, therefore, of importance. (36)

(v)   Follow-up checks on the functioning of the system are useful, e.g. to check whether tenants can still operate the alarm, whether it functions properly, or to identify problems. (99) A common one is for tenants to tie the alarm pull cords up out of the way - indicating poor positioning. (36, 73)

The main study concluded that alarm systems available at the time were far from satisfactory. Since then improvements and new developments have taken place. Of particular interest is the introduction in some schemes of speech systems. (2, 68) However, no evaluation of such systems is available yet. A study conducted by the Building Research Station is currently in progress and should be available soon.

Noise

There has been little research into the problem of noise in sheltered housing and none relating to structural noise insulation. Two studies in which respondents were asked whether they were bothered by noise found that the majority (about three quarters) were not bothered. (31, 73) Of those who were bothered about one-third mentioned external noise sources as the problem and the remainder mentioned either noise from neighbours (e.g. deaf tenants with loud radio/TV) or from the heating system (particularly from warm air systems). Noise from circulation areas has also been noted, and the inclusion of a lobby in the flat design suggested as one way of reducing the impact of this noise. (79)

Lift/stair access   (ADR 5.6.3; 5.6.4; 5.6.6)

Lifts are regarded as essential for schemes with three storeys and over, but are not considered in most schemes of only two storeys. The omission of a lift is supported by the findings in one study that even among residents over 80 years old more than half can manage one flight of stairs. (34) Where lifts have been installed on two storey schemes the installation has usually been justified for occasional or emergency use (10), but they can be heavily used, particularly if there is a high proportion of the frail elderly at the first floor level. (45)

The assumed resistance by the elderly to high storey flats and the use of lifts is not supported by the research. One study found that lifts were well liked and used and that maintenance standards where higher than in ordinary flats because of the smaller amount of mis-use. (32)

Stair (and balcony) access to first floor flats is generally

196

only criticised when there is a lack of shelter. (73) The entrances to first floor flats should be at the first floor level, and not at the foot of the stairs, to remove the necessity of going downstairs to answer the door. (35) American experience suggests that in the interests of security stair accesses should be visible from the outside. (68)

Other internal design   (e.g. ADR 5.1.11; 5.1.12; 5.4.4; 5.6.7; 6.7-6.13)

There are a large number of minor design features which have been researched and implemented in schemes (e.g. location and height of electric points; meters readable from outside dwelling, design and position of door knobs, etc.). The most important of these features from the point of view of safety and comfort have been covered elsewhere, and it was not felt necessary to dwell further on the remaining minor features.

Warden's unit   (ADR 3.2; 5.1.2; 5.1.3; 5.1.4; 6.18)

There has been little research into wardens' evaluations of their accommodation, although it is possible to outline the possible requirements of wardens from recommendations made in the literature. These requirements are for:

(i)   A self-contained dwelling with 'reasonable' privacy, possibly separate from the scheme. (1, 32)
(ii)   The dwelling should be adequate in size for a married warden, i.e. two bedroomed dwelling at least. (1)
(iii)   The warden should not be expected to use part of the private dwelling as an office; an office should preferably be away from the flat. (1, 6, 35)
(iv)   Relief wardens should not have to use the resident warden's flat. (1)
(v)   The scheme should contain extra storage facilities for any communal equipment used by the warden.
(vi)   The warden should have a garage, and a telephone. (1)

There is a divergence of ideas as to whether the wardens' accommodation should be on the ground floor (Hanover recommendation) or on the first floor of two storey schemes (partly for reasons of privacy). (35) The suggestion that the

197

warden's flat should be central (35) has to be matched against the needs of privacy for the warden. In either case, the flat should be linked to the scheme by a covered and heated corridor. (79)

Communal areas   (ADR 5.1.1; 6.19)

The type of communal facilities provided in sheltered housing schemes varies considerably with the size, function, and ownership of the schemes. The need for communal facilities also varies with the amount of facilities already provided in the neighbourhood. (43)   The most frequently provided facilities, and the ones which are discussed in this section, are guest bedrooms, laundry and drying rooms, and common rooms.

Guest room   The role of guest rooms in sheltered housing varies from that of a 'spare bedroom' for the use of tenants' casual visitors, to that of a room for the use of relatives, friends or nursing staff in the case of a tenant being ill. The use to which a guest room is put, therefore, depends to a large extent on the restrictions made on its use as well as the ease with which it can be used (e.g. location, booking procedures, cost, etc.). (56)

Generally, even where there are few restrictions and only a nominal charge is made for the use of the guest room the rate of usage is low (e.g. only 9 per cent of tenants used it in one set of schemes studied. (31, 32)) When this facility is not provided it often is not missed (32) or the demand for it is low. (10) This is particularly the case where there is space for a spare bed within the tenant's dwelling and where day visits predominate.

The utility of a guest room can be increased if it is adaptable for other uses, e.g. for the relief warden, or for small meetings. (1, 35)   Without these additional uses provision of a guest room appears to have a low priority on the evidence reviewed.

Laundry/drying rooms   Laundry and drying facilities, where provided, are more heavily used than guest rooms; not surprising in view of the fact that washing is an essential household function. Previous research indicates that over a half of the tenants in sheltered housing still do their own washing as opposed to sending it to a laundry or to relatives. (31, 32, 56) Although this proportion depends on the age and ability of tenants, it is not so related to the provision of communal laundry facilities.

The use of communal laundry facilities as opposed to the washing being done in the tenant's flat (or launderette) is dependent upon:
- the type of equipment provided - size and simplicity of washing machines (35)
- the numbers of tenants sharing the equipment, and
- the ownership of private washing machines, driers, etc. (73)

Several researchers have noted that drying is more of a problem for tenants than washing, and that indoor drying facilities are appreciated when provided. (31, 56, 73)

In schemes in which no laundry or drying facilities have been provided the demand for such facilities is small, possibly because most tenants have adapted to alternative arrangements. In one study only 17 per cent of those who had no communal facilities said they would like them. (32)

Common room   The opinions as to whether a common room should be provided in sheltered housing schemes vary from 'At least one centrally located community room should be provided' (68) to 'In general, the provision of a common room is not justified by its use'. (73) One problem is that of defining the expected role that a common room should play, and matching this with the residents and wardens in a scheme. The roles assigned to common rooms vary from use as a TV room and casual lounge to a general meeting place used only for special occasions.   The literature relating to schemes having predominantly bedsitting accommodation generally assumes that a common room would be provided and lays down the following recommendations for a common room: central location; linked to warden's flats; should not be a through route; a separate TV room is advisable; not too large; toilet and cooking facilities should be provided or close; should be linked to flats by a covered and heated way. (31, 32,

199

In schemes without a common room a varying proportion (up to half) of the tenants wanted one, although it is not always clear why, or what they perceived as the function of a common room. (10, 53) The requirement for some place where tenants can meet if they wish has been noted, but this function can be fulfilled by other spaces in a scheme as well as a common room providing the design is suitable. (5, 10)

An institutional appearance can be avoided in these circulation spaces by sensitive attention to design particularly with regard to furniture, so that informal social contact is given encouragement. (8, 43)

It is not possible to draw any firm conclusions about the provision of common rooms because of the number of factors which have not been included in previous research, e.g. characteristics of tenants, wardens, role of scheme socially, provision of facilities in the neighbourhood, etc.

Other communal facilities A variety of other facilities have been included in schemes or mentioned in the research, e.g. hobbies room, coffee shops, shops, public telephones, storage space, health centres, etc. Generally, such facilities, with the exception of public telephones, for example, are only viable on large schemes of over c. 100 tenants. (32, 43, 68) Alternatively, such services could be made available to the wider community.

Only a small proportion of tenants have their own phones (35) and public telephones are popular when included in a scheme. In one study 57 per cent of tenants used the telephone when it was installed, and 42 per cent of those without one would like one installed in the scheme. (3)

Few schemes in the UK have included shops, but they are apparently well used in those schemes which have them. (32)

EXTERNAL ASPECTS

In contrast to the relatively detailed guidelines for internal design, the external design of the site and buildings have received little attention in research beyond comments on obvious extreme cases. This will become clear as the aspects are dealt with in turn, as will the number of untested assumptions about the elderly and their preferences.

Site, size and aspect (ADR 1, 2)

The size of the site, and hence the size of the scheme, is usually determined by a number of factors, but primarily the availability of land in the desired location. However, there is no evidence to suggest that the size has any relationship with tenants' satisfaction. (32, 57)

Two main suggestions appear in the reseach regarding the size and aspect of the site, although neither have been rigorously tested:

(i)   The size should not be too large, so as to give the impression of separation from the community. (35) Hanover site requirements suggest 0.25-0.6 hectares as the norm (150 bed spaces/hectare minimum). It is clear, however, that size of site is only one factor in the complex issue of 'separation' or 'belonging' to a community and secondary to factors such as family ties of tenants, life styles, etc. (69)

(ii)   'Backland' should be avoided. (35) This is based on an extension of the first point, i.e. avoiding situations where the elderly have nothing to watch and no contact with the surrounding community. However, the distinction between 'interesting action' and 'disturbing activity' is not easy to define. This factor is also less important for the more active elderly who can seek their action in the normal way if they so wish. (73)

Privacy (ADR 4.3; 4.8; 4.11)

The privacy of the site appears to be one of the most critical external aspects of sheltered housing, and yet it is not so much a function of the location of the site as of the layout. (73) The dogma of integrating the elderly into the community is not supported in the research; in general, privacy and

201

seclusion are sought after - 'not isolation, but insulation'. (13, 56, 73)

The design features which should be considered in connection with privacy are:

(i)   Avoidance of public footpaths crossing the site and the discouragement of the use of the site as a short-cut, (56, 68, 90)   This may mean the erection of physical barriers in some cases, or the routing of paths at right angles to the site axis for example. (6)

(ii)   The use of low fences or shrubs to delineate the site and discourage intrusion. Alternatively, the building structure itself could be used as the barrier. (68, 73)

(iii)   Making site areas easily visible to staff and residents. The extension of 'personal space' into the grounds tends to enhance people's responsibility for what occurs there. (43, 68)

(iv)   Avoidance of siting where overlooking or intrusion is likely, e.g alongside higher-rise developments; childrens' playgounds, etc. (73)

Security

The security of the site is an extension of privacy, except that it is more concerned with the physical control or prevention of unwanted entry to the site rather than deterring occasional intrusion. This aspect of site design is strongly emphasised in American literature, but has not featured much in research in the UK (except possibly with reference to vandalism). The suggested design features for US schemes include restricting entry to a single front door with a security guard or front door buzz lock; high outdoor illumination and TV screening of the entrance. (43, 68)

Evidence in the UK suggests that completely open access staircases and landings with no outer doors are not liked by residents. In addition, residents on some schemes have been found to want additional security features on their own front doors. (73) This implies that security considerations are of significance, particularly in high risk areas. Further research is required before it is possible to say whether the measures suggested for US schemes would be appropriate.

202

Layout

Two aspects of layout have received attention in the research reviewed (in addition to the purely economic and design considerations of layout):

(i) The number and placing of the buildings and the effect that may have on social contacts among the elderly. Division of a scheme into separate blocks can have an effect by tending to compartmentalise social groups. (73) Spacing the blocks may make the warden's job more difficult, and if communal facilities are also split up the amount of use of the facilities may be affected. Placing of the blocks also has an influence on the privacy of the scheme.

(ii) Space around the building: there has been a general trend in sheltered housing away from providing private garden space to more open planning. This is partly a response to the problems of upkeep of gardens which tenants can no longer maintain. (31, 90) The appearance aspect of open layout is discussed in the next section, but retaining some areas for private gardens can have advantages, e.g. to increase the privacy of the site (73) and to increase tenants' responsibilitues for what happens in the garden areas. (68) A small garden of only five square yards is suggested in one study as satisfying all but the most enthusiastic gardeners. (56) Certainly, a demand for gardens exists. (73) but it should also be recognised that other solutions may exist - raised beds and tubs, for example, to avoid the necessity of stooping (35) - and that the issues of maintenance of a garden if the tenant cannot manage it is of paramount importance.

Appearance   (ADR 4.4; 4.5; 4.6)

There is very little research or guidance on external appearance of schemes, although it is clearly important to tenants (60 per cent of tenants had adverse comments on the layout and appearance of their schemes in the previous Hanover study). (73) What evidence there is suggests that there are two opposing requirements: variety versus

203

maintenance, i.e. it may be desirable to provide landscaped gardens with flower-beds, but this brings problems of cost and maintenance. In schemes where the local parks department are responsible for the grounds a high standard of landscaping has been achieved. (31) In other schemes easy maintenance considerations have resulted in a predominance of plain areas of grass, with some tree planting. Some research emphasises the need to retain an 'open outlook' so that local activity can be seen. (35) American work emphasises the security aspects and recommends that planting be kept without bounds. (68) The standard of upkeep of any landscaping which exists remains one of the most critical factors, and often determines the subsequent fate of such private gardens initially provided. (73)

Paths (ADR 4.9; 4.10; 4.12)

Apart from the issue of the use of paths by the public the main considerations stem basically from commonsense, e.g. avoidance of steep slippery-surface paths, no steps, sufficient width for wheelchair users to pass, adequate lighting at night, avoidance of vehicular contact, lowered kerb at road crossing points, etc. (7)

Clothes drying (ADR 4.3)

Drying of clothes is one of the main problems for tenants, particularly in schemes without drying rooms. (73) The large proportion of tenants doing their own washing has already been noted. There is no basic research into clothes drying areas, but the following problems are mentioned in the research:

(i)   The amount of space per person, e.g. Hanover recommend one rotary drier per six flats, but there is no evidence to indicate whether this is sufficient.

(ii) The distance of the drying area from the flats. (73)

(iii) The privacy of the drying area and the ability to keep washing under surveillance by the tenants. (56, 68, 73)

Outdoor seating (ADR 4.7)

The demand for outdoor seating in schemes for the elderly is fairly high - over a half of the tenants interviewed in two studies liked to sit out in the summer, particularly where privacy existed. (31, 73) A further third of the tenants in one of these studies was not attracted by the idea of sitting out. (73)

Although there is agreement that some sort of outdoor seating should be provided there are mixed opinions about whether the seating should be fixed or whether portable seats should be available. The general fear with fixed outdoor seating is that they may be used by the general public, or could give the scheme an 'institutional' appearance. (73)

Further aspects mentioned in the literature are that the seating should be located with some privacy, but with the maximum possible view of any local activity. In addition, solitary fixed seats as well as the normal benches should possibly be provided for those tenants who do not wish to mix. (68)

Car parking (ADR 4.13; 4.14)

The need for car parking space is relatively low in sheltered housing schemes for the elderly; in the previous Hanover study only 11 per cent of tenants owned a car. (73) This figure varies markedly from scheme to scheme, and, of course, over time. However, at the present, local planning standards require in general for more parking space to be provided than necessary. The Hanover guidelines suggest one parking space for two flats.

Apart from the amount of space provided there are two further points:-

(i) How many garages or car ports to provide, if any? In the Hanover study only one third of the garages provided were being rented by tenants. (73) On the other hand in some schemes no covered or secured parking was provided at all. The basic problem is to cater for these variations in car ownership, as garage provision is inflexible generally.

(ii)   The areas of unused parking space 'invite' intrusion and use by non-residents, i.e. there are problems of control or of alternative use of parking areas.

Other external features   (ADR 5.1.7; 5.6.2)

The other main external feature which is referred to in the literature is the position and nature of refuse disposal facilities. The main problem arising was that of ease of use - for example, the distance tenants had to go to dustbins, poor positioning (too near flats) or poor arrangements (e.g. tenants having to manhandle bins before collection). (73)

There is no mention of any research into other refuse disposal methods in sheltered housing in the literature, and the Hanover Design Requirements cover the basic requirements of convenience and security.

LOCATIONAL ASPECTS

The topic of location of sheltered housing schemes for the elderly is of prime importance, and yet there has been little original research into tenants' satisfaction or needs with respect to location, or into the behavioural demands of the elderly. Most of the research reviewed here has included reference to residents' reactions to specific site locations, but no systematic study taking other important factors than location into account (e.g. characteristics of tenants, desired behaviour, the effect of providing alternative on-scheme facilities, etc.) has yet been done.

A major piece of work is currently under way at the Transport and Road Research Laboratory into the travel behaviour of the elderly compared with a control group of ordinary housewives. (108) When this study is completed (in late summer 1976) it should throw some light on locational requirements of housing schemes. The other major work which relates to this topic is that done by Meyer Hillman, et. al. (54, 55) into the mobility of the elderly and the handicapped.

It is useful at this point to use Hillman's research in order to outline the characteristics of the elderly as they influence the locational requirements of housing schemes.

Firstly, the elderly are more likely than other groups in the population to be on low incomes. They, therefore, have a lower ability to pay for motorised transport, especially cars.

Secondly, the elderly are also more likely to be less physically able - not only to walk, but to use buses or drive cars. Very few of those who are not able to walk are able to use buses.

Thirdly, the pedestrian environment is extremely important for the elderly. In Hillman's study (55) walking was the most widely used mode of transport - 71 per cent of pensioners' trips to shop are on foot; 75 per cent go on foot to collect pensions and over 50 per cent of employed pensioners go to work on foot.

Fourthly, buses are used mainly by those without cars and without local facilities - and these elderly tend to live in the low density areas peripheral to towns. The pricing of the buses is an important issue in this respect as well as the location of schemes.

With these points in mind, and particularly the importance of walking as a mode of travel, the various locational criteria will be discussed in turn.

Town centre

The term town centre is rather loose, and it is not always clear as to what facilities in the centre are either offered, or are in demand by the elderly. The general assumption made in the literature is that all the necessary facilities (e.g. shopping, banking, leisure and social facilities) are located there. Some of these are dealt with in detail separately below.

It is not surprising that no general conclusions have been

drawn in the research as to the desirable location of schemes with respect to town centres, particularly in view of the number of factors involved. A number of useful conclusions have been drawn however:

(i)   Location with respect to the centre represents a trade-off between the cost and availability of sites for schemes, and the travel and servicing convenience. (68)   In addition, the environment changes from an urban one to a suburban or even rural one which may be important to some.

(ii)   In general, the more isolated a scheme is, the more self-sufficient residents have to be. Car ownership, cheap or free bus travel or local service centres can compensate for the actual distance in miles from the centre. (73, 90)

No definitive statement can be made because of the number of variables involved. Only in one study has a relationship between location of scheme and satisfaction been found: in this study tenants on peripheral estates were less satisfied than those nearer the town centre with regard to factors like the cost of bus fares and availability of shops and social amenities.

Shops

Shopping, with foodshops, chemists and post offices as the main shops used, is one of the most frequent external activities of the elderly. (73)   For example, in one study 70 per cent of the elderly in the schemes studied went shopping 3-4 times a week. (53)   Access to shops is thus important, but it cannot be measured just in terms of distance, for prices, physical barriers to movement, bus services, etc. must also be taken into account.   High prices often make local shops less attractive, and habit may also lead the elderly to use shops near their previous homes rather than the nearest ones. (53) Recommended minimum distances to shops are thus likely to be of only limited use because of the simplistic nature of such a standard.   Hanover recommend locating schemes within $\frac{1}{4}$ mile of shops and post office, and the previous Hanover study suggests they should be within 10-30 minutes walk, which to some extent takes the physical problems of getting to shops (e.g. slopes) into account. (73)

Mobile shops have been found to play an important part in shopping habits in some schemes, and particularly for those tenants with restricted mobility. (32, 90)

One response to poor location with respect to shops is the inclusion of a shop within the scheme and this facility has been found to be well used. (32, 68) However, this facility is probably only viable in schemes over a certain size.

Bus

There has been a considerable amount of research into the ability of the elderly to use buses (e.g. factors of bus design) (19) and the effects of bus pricing policies on the use by the elderly of buses. (63) Little of this research is related to the location of schemes with respect to bus routes or bus stops. After walking the use of buses is the most frequent mode of travel for the elderly, and on shopping trips the bus is often used for the return journey after tenants have walked to the shops. (73) Thus, buses are of importance, but as with shopping the distance to the nearest bus stop is not the only locational consideration.

For example, it has been found that the walking distance to the bus stop is a secondary consideration to the waiting time at the bus stop - particularly if the stop is exposed or no seating is provided. (42) Thus, a regular and reliable bus service may be of greater importance than a close stop (Hanover recommend a maximum distance of $\frac{1}{4}$ mile to a regular bus route).

The provision of transport for the scheme itself, or the extension or diversion of bus routes to the scheme, are other possibilities which would imply a degree of organisation (and cost) which most sheltered housing schemes could not support. The provision of scheme transport is recommended in the US if the regular bus is further than 2-4 blocks away. (68)

Church

In certain circumstances a church can be a secondary essential location criterion alongside shopping facilities. This is partly due to the church services themselves, also to the social activities associated with churches. It has been found in some schemes that the church is a much used resource,

(i)   if it is close, and
(ii)   if alternative facilities (either in or near the scheme) are not available. (68)

The previous Hanover study found that 32 per cent of the social activities of the elderly in the schemes were associated with a church. (73) This link is more important for those tenants who previously lived in the area and had already established connections with the church. (57)

Distance guidelines are difficult to specify (although Hanover recommend schemes to be within $\frac{1}{4}$ mile of a church) because of the different functions churches play for tenants, e.g. religious versus social roles, and because of the existence of different denominations which may render a convenient church unacceptable to a tenant. In view of this an ideal location with respect to churches is unlikely to be found, and it is probable that close contact with various churches is of equal importance to close location.

Environmental considerations

Up to the present there has been little original research into the location of schemes for the elderly with respect to sources of noise, pollution, danger, severance, etc. References in the literature have mainly been based on the evaluation of problems at particular schemes, or the application of 'common-sense'. Three main environmental considerations can be identified: noise, safety and barriers to movement.

Noise   The problem of disturbance by noise is generally caused by internal noise (e.g. in the previous Hanover study only 38 per cent of noise complaints related to external noise sources - traffic and children) except in schemes located

210

close to specific noise sources. (7, 73) Two noise sources are of importance: traffic, which tends to affect schemes located in town centres most (5); and children. The location of a sheltered housing scheme near a school, although it may bring useful contacts between the two, poses a major problem of noise, and also intrusion. (35, 68)

Safety   This aspect of location has received even less attention in research short of recommendations about avoiding major roads and road junctions, etc. The Institute for Consumer Ergonomics, Loughborough, is currently investigating the safety hazards to the elderly from traffic, and this research should be reported in 1977. (40)

Barriers to movement   Barriers to the easy movement of the elderly from a scheme can reduce the accessibility of local facilities despite their nearness to the scheme. The most frequently mentioned barriers are steep slopes and major roads which have to be crossed. (35, 68, 73) Poor condition of pavements, or complete lack of pavements, slippery surfaces, steps or kerbs (for those who are wheelchair bound) can also act to reduce the effective accessibility of facilities. (68)

Subways and bridges provided to cross main roads are often unsuitable for use by the elderly either because of their physical design (steep slopes or steps) or their nature (e.g. resulting in fears of attack in a subway).

It is difficult to evaluate the above considerations in assessing a proposed location because of the lack of quantified data available. For the present, at least, the commonsense approach would appear to be necessary.

Other locational considerations

Other local facilities which have been mentioned in the literature as being important are a postal box (often distant on new estates), public telephone (if not provided within the scheme), medical and social services. (73) The latter services are perhaps less important because the service tends to come to the tenant as well as vice versa. The lack of certain facilities near the scheme (e.g. telephone, day centre, health service, etc.) is usually compensated for by the provision of the facility or some alternative within the scheme. In other words, a balance of local and scheme facilities is reached.

The social aspect of location is also important, and many writers have stressed the need either to be integrated with, or separated from the local community (see External Aspects - Privacy and 30, 69). One important factor is the origin of the tenants and the location of the scheme with respect to their former homes and their families. (57, 73) All round social participation has been found to be considerably higher in schemes with the highest proportion of tenants originating from the same area. (73) A high proportion of the elderly move to be near relatives, and much of their visiting is subsequently to and from relatives. The significance of this in terms of location is that there is likely to be a need for sheltered housing both in established residential areas for the local elderly who wish to move from old or large dwellings, and in new areas to cater for those moving to be near relatives. The implications for tenant selection will be referred to later.

MANAGEMENT ASPECTS

The management aspects of sheltered housing revolve mainly around the role of the wardens, and the links of communication between the three main bodies involved in sheltered housing, i.e. the tenants, the wardens and the owning or managing body. There are two main sources of information on this aspect of sheltered housing. The first is the Report of the Age Concern Working Party (1972) into the Role of the Warden in Grouped Housing which forms the basis of current recommendations on conditions of service for wardens. (1) The committee commented on the lack of basic information on wardens and sheltered housing and since then one major survey of the warden's role has been completed (14, 16), and this is the second main source of information which has been drawn upon in this section.

Warden's duties

The role of the warden varies with the scope and character of different sheltered housing schemes, and with this variation in role there are different hours and conditions of service. In some cases no guidance as to the warden's functions is given to the warden. (16, 31) The Age Concern Working Party felt it necessary to lay down some guidelines to enable a greater uniformity in provision and in duties to be achieved. (1) At the same time they recognised the need for flexibility, and suggested that the guidelines would serve as a basis from which adequate recompense to the wardens for additional duties could be calculated. The working party divided the warden's duties into four categories which have been retained for convenience:

General supervision of tenants and property The supervision of the tenants really implies that the warden acts as a 'good neighbour' whose aim is to underline rather than undermine the independence and relative normality of the tenants. (1) Although the working party recommend that daily visits to tenants were not necessary and should be at the discretion of the warden a quarter of the wardens interviewed in Boldy's study were required to make a daily visit to each tenant. (16)

The supervision of property includes both clerical and manual aspects, from the keeping of records to mending fuses. In some cases the warden has to collect rents, but this task can impair the function of the warden in other spheres, e.g. as the good neighbour and the working party advised against rent collection being undertaken by the wardens. (1) Other problems related to the property are defining what repairs the warden (or the warden's spouse) can be expected to do, and the amount of maintenance and cleaning they should carry out. Boldy found that 20 per cent of the warden's time was spent on housekeeping and administration on average, but that in some cases wardens were having to undertake unreasonably large amounts of cleaning. (16) Not surprisingly, therefore, 25 per cent of wardens disliked their cleaning tasks. The recommendation which arises from this is that where there were large amounts of cleaning (e.g. over 12 hours per week) there should be either extra recompense for the warden, or additional physical help.

General assistance This category of duties was made by the working party because it was felt that the warden had certain duties to provide assistance to tenants as required, e.g.

213

shopping, collection of pensions and medicines, advice and temporary domestic help. One major problem here is in defining what is properly the function of domiciliary services or relatives and what the wardens should or can do. This is particularly difficult in cases of temporary domestic help, the main problem being in defining the term 'temporary'. Obviously, the capacity of the warden to undertake general assistance duties will vary with the number of tenants per warden which varies in the range 20-90 tenants per warden, although 30 has been recommended as a suitable size. (32, 79)

Boldy found that on average wardens spent two thirds of their time on general support to tenants; of which half was regular visiting and over a quarter was spent on temporary functions, e.g shopping and cooking. (16) He suggests that more wardens exceeded their brief in this duty, and problems of involvement with tenants could interfere with their other functions. In this respect the need to inform tenants and their relatives of the limits of the warden's functions has to be recognised. (1, 73)

Emergency duties The provision of manned alarm systems is one of the distinctive features of sheltered housing schemes. However, to be effective the system has to be monitored for 24 hours a day every day of the week - and it is clearly unreasonable to expect one person to do this. Yet in Boldy's survey of wardens only a half were specifically given time off and hence provision made for a temporary replacement. (16) Some wardens found they could not leave their schemes for more than an hour without worrying. In the same study the average time spent dealing with emergency calls was 10 per cent of the total, averaging less than one call per week.

The Age Concern Working Party felt that it was reasonable to expect the warden to have two days off per week, and to have a working week of less than 40 hours. The provision of a deputy is, therefore, important. In many schemes the wardens are expected to arrange holiday and day-off reliefs themselves, resulting in extreme cases in wardens preferring not to take a holiday to save the bother of finding a relief. Another problem in some schemes is the necessity of the holiday relief using the warden's own flat because the alarm system is located there. (1, 20) The working party recommended that the finding of a relief should not be the warden's task, and that separate accommodation for a relief was vital to retain the privacy of the warden's home.

Group social activities   On average wardens interviewed by Boldy spent only 5 per cent of their time on organising communal activities, although this rose to 13 per cent on average for those schemes with common rooms. (16)   The working party felt that the warden should have 'a general duty to foster and protect the happy atmosphere of the group as a whole'. (1)   This duty they point out should be coupled with the right of a tenant not to participate.

It has been shown that tenants in wardened schemes are more closely integrated with their neighbours and in attendance at social functions.   However, this integration is at the expense of informal contacts outside the scheme.   The danger with this is that the tenants' cherished independence may in fact be undermined by the provision of extensive social facilities on the scheme. (29, 59)

On the other hand the warden can be of prime importance in maintaining tenants' contact with the outside world.   In both cases, there is a great dependence on the warden's ability and it raises the question of training of wardens (see later).

Support for wardens

The issue of deputy wardens has already been mentioned, but there are other sources of support for the wardens - from the employers, welfare services and indeed from other wardens.   The links required with welfare, hospital and doctors' services are not discussed here, but clearly a mutual understanding of each other's roles and limitations is necessary for effective functioning of all services. (1, 43)

Support from the employers is necessary for carrying out repairs and emphasising the warden's role and authority. However, it is also necesssary for them to delegate to the wardens considerable authority in order to make their work effective - particularly in avoiding having to refer to Head Office before making or carrying out any decision.

The working party pointed out that the warden's job is a lonely one, and that 'social support' is required. (1) This may come from the warden's family, but links with other wardens (formal or informal) may be an important channel for solving some problems.

Other matters affecting wardens

Two other important matters were considered by the Age Concern Working Party: training and qualifications of wardens; and their rates of payment and conditions of service.

The working party considered that briefing of the warden on appointment was necessary, rather than any extensive pre-service training. This should, however, be followed by some in-service training. Nursing qualifications were not felt to be necessary. (1)

The wide range of rates of pay and conditions of service in existence was felt by the working party to be undesirable. They recommended that a national payscale be adopted, giving wardens an officer status. The salary should take into account whether accommodation is provided (as in most cases) or not. A further recommendation was for a maximum of a 40 hour week with at least one full day off each week and a further four days in a four week period. (1)

Tenant selection

This can be as important as the selection of the warden in ensuring that the occupants of a scheme are matched to the nature of the scheme. Two main issues are covered in the research: firstly, the capacity of the tenants to lead independent lives; and secondly, the locational aspect of selection.

(i)   The average tenants of sheltered housing are less able than the general elderly population, but there are fewer severely handicapped than in residential homes.

216

(29)   A distinction can be made between the high
initial care group - who would demand hospital or
residential home accommodation normally, and the
low initial care group - who would be more suitable
for sheltered housing. (15) However, the group needs
tend to become more demanding with time, which
implies that the low initial care group will eventually
require considerable warden and other support, and
may even require transfer to more suitable
accommodation. (7, 106)   The proportion of tenants
who present severe difficulties, therefore, tends to
increase as a scheme gets older, putting the warden
under increasing stress. (29)

The relevance of this from the point of view of
selection is to obtain a balance between the fit and
the unfit from the outset, and to use this as a
criterion of selection when replacement occurs later
on. (1)   This may not be possible always, particularly
where   other criteria (e.g. housing need) are of
greater importance. (29)

(ii)   The second issue, which has not received much
attention, except with regard to retirement to
coastal areas (64, 97) is the selection of tenants on
the basis of the familial and social locational ties.
The research on those who retire away from their
original homes and families suggests that   the
'uprooted elderly' tend to be far more dependent upon
local social and medical facilities than the normal
elderly. (97)   In the case of sheltered housing this
burden would tend to fall on the warden. In addition
to the care support required, the 'uprooted elderly'
often experience other psychological problems,
including loneliness.

This evidence suggests that to be successful, and to keep
the warden's task within reasonable limits, sheltered housing
schemes should cater primarily for those who live in the
immediate vicinity, and also those who wish to be with local
relatives. The existence of a set of social relationships in the
locality can have a distinct effect on the needs of the elderly

217

and their ability to remain on a scheme. (73) Indeed, this selection criterion appears to be operating already; in the previous Hanover study the majority of the tenants were found to be locals, or persons who had moved to be near relatives. (73)

APPENDIX II
SELECTIVE BIBLIOGRAPHY OF LITERATURE
AND RESEARCH

(Items are arranged in alphabetical order by author, editor, journal, or researcher)

1.   Age Concern, 'Role of the Warden in Grouped Housing', National Old People's Welfare Council, Mitcham, 1972
2.   Architecture East Midlands, 'Old People's Flats in Derbyshire', Vol..58, Mar./Apr., pp. 39-40, 1975
3.   Architects' Journal, 'Old People's Flatlets, Stevenage', Oct. 13, pp. 873-884, 1965
4.   Architects' Journal, 'Old People's Flats, Leamington Spa', Oct. 13, pp. 873-884, 1965
5.   Architects' Journal, 'Old People's Flats, Aldeburgh, Suffolk' Oct. 20, pp. 917-928, 1965
6.   Architects' Journal, 'Housing for Old People, Cheviot Road, London, S.E.27', Feb. 28,. pp. 495-508, 1968
7.   Architects' Journal, 'Sheltered Housing for Old People at Nuneaton and Faversham', Oct. 3, pp. 787-798, 1973
8.   Architects' Journal, 'Old People's Housing at Tenterden, Kent', May 28, pp. 1127-1138, 1975
9.   Ashford, N., 'A Brief Comparison of the Problem of Elderly Persons', Mobility in the US and the UK', Paper given at Forum on Transport and the Elderly, Beth Johnson Foundation, 1976
10.   Ball, P. and Gibson, M., 'A Study of Elderly Women Living in Flatlets in Large Converted Houses', Sociology Department, University of Liverpool, 1975
11.   Barret, A.N., 'Purpose Built Local Authority Residential Homes for Old People: the notion of domesticity in design', PhD Research, University of Wales Institute of Science and Technology
12.   Berti, J., 'Striving for Homeliness', Built Environment 9, pp. 500-503, 1973
13.   Beyer, G.H. and Nierstrasz, F.H.J., 'Housing the Aged in Western Countries', Elsevier, 1967

14. Boldy, D., 'Summarised Results of a Study of the Duties and Activities of the Wardens of Grouped Dwellings in Devon AC', Institute of Biometry and Community Medicine, Exeter University, 1973

15. Boldy, D. et. al., 'The Elderly in Grouped Dwellings: a profile', Institute of Biometry and Community Medicine Publication 3, Exeter University, 1973

16. Boldy, D., 'Grouped Dwellings in Devon - A Preliminary Report on a Study of Wardens' Duties and Activities', Institute of Biometry and Community Medicine, Interim Report, IR 12, Exeter University, 1973

17. Bone, S., 'Trust Sheltered Housing', Built Environment 9, pp. 504-507, 1973

18. Brearley, C.P., 'Social Work, Ageing and Society', Routledge and Kegan Paul, London, 1975

19. British Leyland UK Ltd., 'An Investigation of Factors Affecting the Use of Buses by both Elderly and Ambulant Disabled Persons', Current Research

20. Burns, J.T. 'Housing the Elderly in Bedworth', Housing Review, March-April, pp. 39-41, 1971

21. Byerts, T.O., 'Housing and Environment for the Elderly - Conference Proceedings', Gerentological Society, Washington, 1973

22. Blythway, W.R., 'Suggestions for Sheltered Housing', Washington, 1973

23. Canvin, R.W. and Pearson, N.G. (eds.) 'Needs of the Elderly for Health and Welfare Services', Institute of Biometry and Community Medicine Publication 2, Exeter University, 1973

24. Carter, P., 'A Morning with the Elderly', District Councils Review, July, pp. 178-79, 1975

25. Central Council for the Disabled, 'Planning for Disabled People in the Urban Environment', The Council, London, 1969

26. Centre on Environment for the Handicapped, 'The Old and the Mentally Ill', 1973

27. Chadwick, H., 'Basic Accommodation for Old People', Architects' Journal, Sept. 6, pp. 340-343, 1961

28. Council for Codes of Practice, 'Access for the Disabled for Buildings, Part 1: General Recommendations', British Standards Institution, 1961

29.   Cox, R.E., 'A Study of Sheltered Housing and its Relation to other Local Authority Services for Old People', M.A. Thesis, Manchester, 1972

30.   Cummings and Henry, 'Growing Old, the Process of Disengagement', Basic Books, 1961

31.   Department of the Environment, 'Grouped Flatlets for Old People: A sociological study', Design Bulletin 2 (Metric Edition), HMSO, 1968

32.   Department of the Environment, 'Housing for the Elderly: the size of grouped dwellings', Design Bulletin 31, HMSO, 1975

33.   Department of the Environment, Circular 92/75, 'Wheelchair and Mobility Housing: Standards and Costs', 1975

34.   Empson, M., 'The Housing Needs of Old People', Architects' Journal, May 11, pp. 697-704, 1961

35.   Empson, M. and Sheppard, N., 'Housing for Old People', (3 parts), Architects' Journal, 19 July, pp. 177-180; 26 July, pp. 237-242; 2 Aug. pp. 295-298, 1967

36.   Feeney, B. et. al., 'Alarm Systems for Elderly and Disabled People', Institute for Consumer Ergonomics, University of Technology, Loughborough, 1975

37.   Feeney, B. et. al., 'An Evaluation of Alarm Systems for the Elderly and Disabled', (2 vols), Institute of Consumer Ergonomics, University of Technology, 1975

38.   Fennell, G., 'A Study of Social Interaction in Grouped Dwellings for the Elderly in Newcastle-upon-Tyne', PhD research, School of Social Studies, University of East Anglia

39.   Fox, D., 'Housing Needs for the Elderly', Housing Monthly, Vol. 10, Nov, pp. 3-4, 6-9, 1974

40.   Galer, I.A.R., 'Road Safety and the Elderly Pedestrian', Current Research at the Institute for Consumer Ergonomics, Loughborough University of Technology

41.   Garden, J., 'Mobility and the Elderly', National Old People's Welfare Council, Mitcham

42.   Garden, J., 'The Urban Mobility Problems of the Elderly', in Changing Directions, The Report of the Independent Commission on Transport, Coronet Books, pp. 315-322, 1974

221

43. Gelwicks, L.E. and Newcomer, R.J., 'Planning Housing Environments for the Elderly', The National Council on the Aging, Washington DC, 1974

44. Goldsmith, S., 'Designing for the Disabled', RIBA, London, 1963

45. Goldsmith, S., 'Accommodation for Old People: Two Schemes at Norwich', Architects' Journal, Jan. 28, pp. 221-232, 1970

46. Goldsmith, S., 'Mobility Housing', Architects' Journal, June 25, pp. 43-50, 1974

47. Goldsmith, S., 'Wheelchair Housing', Architects' Journal, June 25, pp. 1319-1348, 1975

48. Gray, J.A.M., 'Housing for the Elderly', Housing Monthly, Vol. II, July, pp. 28-29, 1975

49. Greater London Conference on Old People's Welfare, 'Wardens of Sheltered Housing Schemes for the Elderly: report of a working party',1970

50. Gregory, P. and Young, M., 'Lifeline Telephone Service for the Elderly, Pilot Project Hull', National Innovations Centre, 1972

51. Guardian, 'Housing for the Elderly: Special Report', The Guardian, April 6, pp. 21-24, 1976

52. Harris, R. and Luck, G.M., 'Care of the Elderly', Tavistock Institute of Human Relations, IOR/717R, 1973

53. Haynes, K.J. and Raven, J., 'Old People: A Study of Living Patterns', Architects' Journal, October 26, pp. 1051-1066, 1966

54. Hillman, M., 'Personal Mobility and Transport Policy', Political and Economic Planning Broadsheet, 542, London, 1973

55. Hillman, M., et. al., 'Mobility and Accessibility in the Outer Metropolitan Area', Extracts from Conclusions of a Report to the Department of the Environment, 1974

56. Hole, V., 'Some Aspects of Housing for Old Persons', Architects' Journal, 20 April, pp. 583-586 and 27 April, pp. 605-6-8, 1961

57. Hole, V. and Allen, P.G., 'A Survey of Housing for Old People', Architects' Journal, May 9, pp. 1017-1026, 1962

58. Hole, V. and Allen, P.G., 'Rehousing Old People', Architects' Journal, Jan. 8, pp. 75-82, 1964

222

59. Horsley, 'Purpose Built Warden Controlled Residential Accommodation for Elderly People', MA Thesis, Bangor College, University of Wales, 1971

60. Housing Review, 'Old People's Housing, Westmill Road, Hitchin, Herts.', March-April, pp. 41-43, 1971

61. Institute of Housing Managers, 'Grouped Dwellings for the Elderly', 1967

62. Isaacs, B. 'Housing for Old People - Medical Aspects', Housing, Vol. 2/2, p. 25, 1966

63. Jenkins, I.A. and Skelton, N.G., 'Some Implications of Fare Concessions for the Elderly', PTRC Summer Meeting, 1975

64. Karn, V.A. 'Retiring to the Seaside: a study of retirement migration in England and Wales', PhD Thesis, University of Birmingham

65. Kemp, M. 'An Update of the Workhouse', Built Environment, 9, pp. 496-497, 1973

66. Korte, S., 'Designing for Old People, the Role of Residential Homes', Architects' Journal, Oct. 19, pp. 987-991, 1966

67. Lawton, M. Powell, 'Planner's Notebook: Planning Environment for Older People', Journal of the American Institute of Planners, March, pp. 124-130, 1970

68. Lawton, M. Powell, 'Planning and Managing Housing for the Elderly', J. Wiley and Sons Inc., New York, 1975

69. Lipman, A. 'Old People's Homes: siting and neighbourhood integration', Sociological Review, Nov., pp. 323-338, 1968

70. Lipman, A., 'Building Design and Social Interaction: a preliminary study of three old people's homes', Architects' Journal, Jan. 3, pp. 23-30, 1968

71. Lomas, G., 'Housing the Elderly', Built Enviroment 9, pp. 491-493, 1973

72. London Borough of Greenwich, 'Old People's Homes and Sheltered Housing in Greenwich', 1972

73. Mercer, D. and Muir, T., 'Hanover Housing Association Assessment Study - Final Report', CURS, University of Birmingham, 1969

74. Michelson, W., 'Man and his Urban Environment: A Sociological Approach', Addison-Wesley, Reading, Mass., 1974

75. Ministry of Housing and Local Government (MHLG), 'Housing of Old People', Circular 55/67, 1957
76. MHLG, 'Flatlets for Old People', HMSO, 1958
77. MHLG, 'More Flatlets for Old People', HMSO, 1960
78. MHLG, 'Some Aspects of Designing for Old People', Design Bulletin 1, HMSO, 1962
79. MHLG, 'Old People's Flatlets in Stevenage, an account of the project with an appraisal', Design Bulletin 11, HMSO, 1969
80. MHLG, 'Housing Standards and Costs - Accommodation Specially Designed for Old People', Circular 82/69, 1969
81. McNab, A., 'Services, Planning and Hardware for the Disadvantaged', Architectural Design 5 (May), pp. 294-301, 1973
82. Municipal and Public Services Journal, 'New Patterns in Homes for the Aged', Oct. 31, pp. 2740-2741, 1969
83. Murphy, P. and Topp, A., 'Condominiums and the Elderly: A convenient marriage or a marriage of convenience', Habitat, Vol. 18/1, pp. 14-16, 1975
84. National Corporation for the Care of Old People, Old Age - A Register of Social Research', NCCOP, London, 1972 onwards
85. National Old People's Welfare Council, 'Accommodation for the Elderly: comments on the adequacy of accommodation for the elderly and suggestions for further development', The Council, Mitcham
86. Noah, E., 'Homes for the Aged: supervision and standards: a report on the legal situation in European countries', US Department of Health, Education and Welfare, Office of Human Development, Washington
87. Page, D. and Muir, T., 'New Housing for the Elderly', National Council of Social Service, 1971
88. Perrett, E., 'Preliminary Report of an Inquiry into the Effectiveness of Sheltered Housing Schemes and their Bearing on the Need for Residential Care', University of Keele, 1969
89. Pianca, M.J., 'Role for Charities', Built Environment, 9, pp. 498-499, 1968
90. Pratt, M.L., 'Borough of Taunton: survey of older person's accommodation with warden service',

Housing, July, pp. 5-12, 1968
91. Rheumatism Research Unit, 'An Evaluation of Certain Bathroom and Toileting Aids and Appliances for the Disabled', University of Leeds - Current Research
92. The Right to Fuel Campaign, 'Action Kit', 1976
93. Royal Society of Health Journal, 'Care of the Elderly' (several articles), Vol. 95, April, pp. 83-102, 1975
94. School of Architecture and Urban Planning, 'The Built Environment for the Elderly, research report', Princeton University, NJ
95. Scottish Development Department, 'Housing for Old People with Design Standards for the Disabled', Edinburgh, HMSO, 1970
96. Simmie, J.M., 'Housing and the Elderly: A Study of Walton Manor, Oxford', Journal of the Royal Town Planning Institute, Sept.-Oct., pp. 350-352, 1969
97. Skrimshire, John, 'Retiring to the Seaside', Built Environment, pp. 494-495, 1973
98. Smith, 'Housing Problems of Older Persons -The Management Point of View', Housing 2/2, p. 18, 1966
99. Social Services and Intelligence Unit, 'Alarms for the Elderly and Disabled in Portsmouth', The Unit, Occasional Paper No. 5, Portsmouth, 1975
100. Stubbs, H., 'Housing for the Elderly', House Builder, Vol, 35, July 1975
101. Sumner, G. and Smith, R., 'Planning Local Authority Services for the Elderly', George Allen and Unwin Ltd., London, 1969
102. Sumner, G., 'Priorities and Policies in Accommodation: the contribution that sheltered housing can make', Conference on the National Housing Societies and Scottish Old People's Welfare Committee, 1970
103. Thomas, R., 'Grouped Flats/Flatlets for Old People: a study of problems experienced by tenants in connection with dwelling design', PhD Research, UWIST, Cardiff
104. Thompson, Q.L., 'Assessing the Need for Residential Care for the Elderly', GLC Intelligence Unit Quarterly, No. 24, Sept., pp.37-42, 1973
105. Townsend, C., 'Old Age, the last segregation', Grossman, NY, 1971

225

106. Townsend, P., 'The Needs of the Elderly and the Planning of Hospitals', in Canvin, R.W. and Pearson, N. (eds.), 'Needs of the Elderly', op. cit. pp. 47-70
107. Townsend, P., 'The Last Refuge: A Survey of Residential Institutions and Homes for the Aged in England and Wales', Routledge and Kegan Paul, London, 1964
108. Transport and Road Research Laboratory, Access and Mobility Division (1974-76) 'Aspects of the Mobility of Old People', Current Research
109. Tunstall, J., 'Old and Alone', Routledge and Kegan Paul, London, 1966
110. Wager, R. 'Care of the Elderly - an Exercise in Cost Benefit Analysis', Institute of Municipal Treasurers and Accountants, London, 1972
111. Webb, M.M., 'A Review of Housing for the Elderly', in Urban Renewal 73, ed. S. Millward, pp. 91-108, 1973
112. Werk, 'Alter wohnungen', No. 7, pp. 639-674, July
113. Which, 'Heating and the Poor', July 1974
114. Wilner, D.M. and Walkley, R.P., 'Some Special Problems and Alternatives in Housing for Older Persons', in McKinner, J.C. and de Vyver, F.T., 'Aging and Social Policy', Appleton - Century Crofts, NY, pp. 221-259, 1966

Additional North American References

115. Barker, Michael, B., 'California Retirement Opportunities', Center for Real Estate and Urban Economics, Institute of Urban and Regional Development, University of Carolina, Berkeley, 1966
116. Environics Research Group Ltd.. 'The Elderly and their Environment: a pilot study into Senior Citizens' Housing Satisfaction', Study prepared for CMHC, Canada, 1971
117. Hamovitch, M.B., Peterson, J.A. and Larson, A.E., 'Perception and Fulfillment of Housing Needs of an Aging Population', University of Southern California Gerentology Center, 1969
118. Jacobs, Jerry, 'Older Persons and Retirement Communities', Springfield, Charles T. Thomas, 1975
119. Kassabaum, George, 'Housing the Elderly - Technical

Standards of Design', AIA Journal, September 1962

120. Lawton, M. Powell, 'Public Behaviour of Older People in Congregate Housing', Philadelphia Gerentology Centre

121. Noam, Ernst, 'Homes for the Aged: Supervision and Standards', A report on the legal situation in European Countries. Translated from German by John S. Marks. Washington: US Department of Health, Education and Welfare, Office of Human Developent, Administration on Aging, National Clearinghouse on Aging, DHEW Publication No. (OHD) 75-20104, 1975

122. 'Adult Day Facilities for Treatment, Health, Care and Related Services', A Working Paper, prepared by the Special Committee on Aging. US Senate, Washington: US Government Printing Office, 72-862, 1976